IMAGES ·
of America

KENNEBUNK

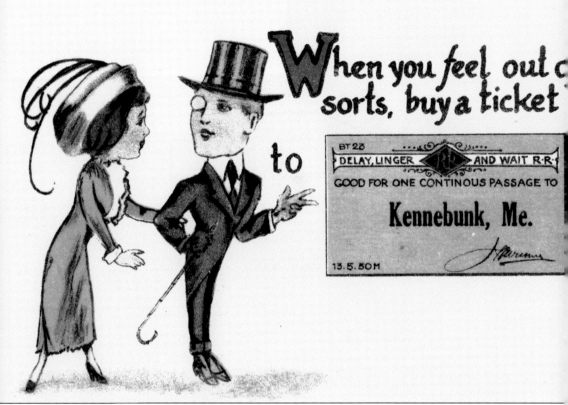

AN INVITATION TO KENNEBUNK. This 1910 postcard beckons travelers to visit Kennebunk.

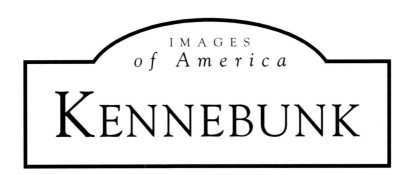

IMAGES
of America

KENNEBUNK

Kathleen Ostrander

ARCADIA
PUBLISHING

Copyright © 2005 by Kathleen Ostrander
ISBN 978-0-7385-3714-6

Published by Arcadia Publishing
Charleston, South Carolina

Printed in the United States of America

Library of Congress Catalog Card Number: 2004113463

For all general information, contact Arcadia Publishing:
Telephone 843-853-2070
Fax 843-853-0044
E-mail sales@arcadiapublishing.com
For customer service and orders:
Toll-free 1-888-313-2665

Visit us on the Internet at www.arcadiapublishing.com

CONTENTS

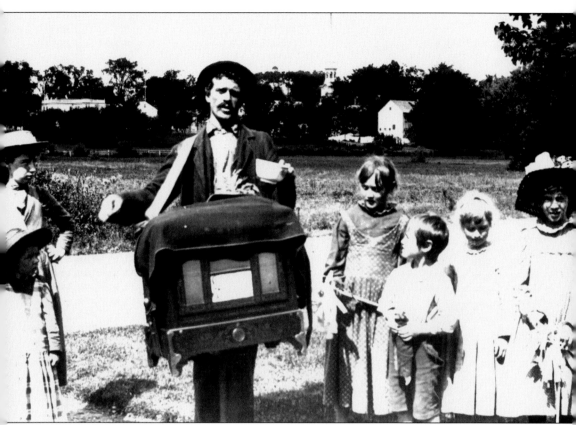

EARLY ENTERTAINMENT. An organ grinder is shown entertaining children at the corner of Park and Dane Streets in Kennebunk at the turn of the 20th century. Upon arriving in America, some immigrants accepted offers to lease hand organs from various firms in New York City. The immigrants then could earn a meager wage by traveling about and charging money to play melodies on the portable organs. (85.L.70.)

INTRODUCTION

What would the early settlers of Kennebunk think if they were able to come back and see the changes in our area since 1643? What would the residents of 100 years ago think if they could visit once more? Would anything be recognizable to them? Would settler Stephen Larrabee be able to look at the curves of the Mousam River and tell us precisely where he built his garrison and why he chose that location?

As our town grows and changes, the locations known to residents 300 years ago become obscured by progress. Written histories of the Kennebunks, such as those authored by E. E. Bourne and Daniel Remich, although fascinating, are hard to visualize since no photographs graced their pages. The photographic process developed in the mid-1850s enables us to actually see what Kennebunk looked like 100 years ago and makes our history more tangible.

Kennebunk is fortunate to have a repository for its historic artifacts, photographs, and documents. The Brick Store Museum, founded in 1939 by Edith Barry, is a treasure trove of local history. The museum's collection includes belongings of our town's ancestors, images of what those people looked like, handwritten documents, examples of clothing they wore, and weapons and tools they used. All of these things are available to help bridge the distance between past and present.

With this book I hope to bring you visually one step closer to the past. The majority of the images used in this book are from the archives of the Brick Store Museum. Each image belonging to the Brick Store Museum is identified by archive location numbers in parentheses following the caption. I have tried to focus on certain sections of our town, such as the in-town neighborhoods, the Landing, Lower Village, West Kennebunk, and Alewive. Because a previous book from Arcadia already has focused on Main Street Kennebunk, I have included fewer images of that area. Also, I have not focused on Kennebunk Beach because a previous book on this subject has been written by Rosalind Magnuson. Space constraints have allowed me to share only a fraction of the photographs that exist at the Brick Store Museum.

It is my hope that this book will inspire people to visit the Brick Store Museum, at 117 Main Street in Kennebunk, and see for themselves the magnitude of local history available within its archives.

Enjoy!

—Kathleen Ostrander

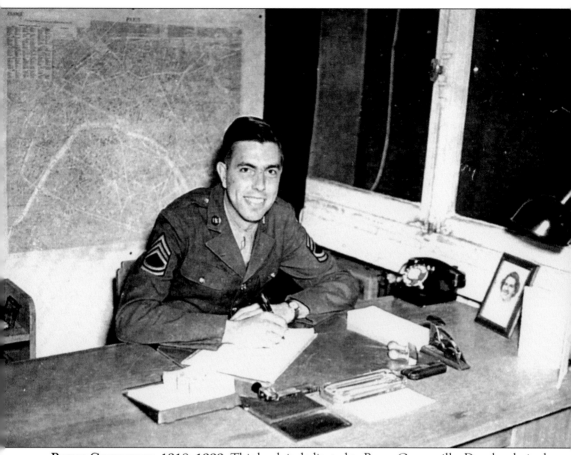

ROGER GONNEVILLE, 1918–1999. This book is dedicated to Roger Gonneville. Deeply admired and sadly missed.

One

THE EARLY YEARS

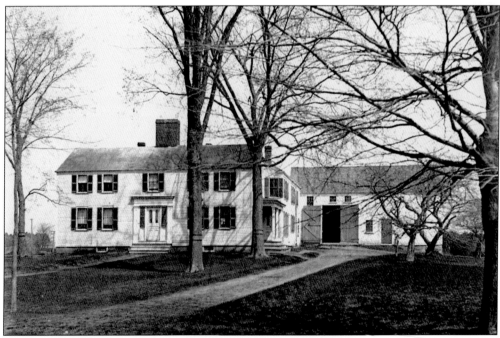

CAPT. JAMES HUBBARD HOUSE. This home built *c.* 1750 at 56 Summer Street is one of the oldest houses in Kennebunk. Captain Hubbard died in the Revolutionary War at Cambridge in 1776. The barn that was once attached by an ell to the main house has been separated, moved back, and remodeled into a home. (84.L.190.)

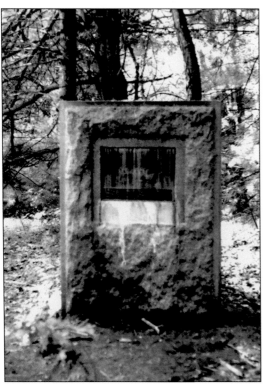

LARRABEE GARRISON MONUMENT. In 1908 historian William Barry placed this monument on the site of the original Larrabee Garrison, which is known to be one of the earliest settlements on the Mousam River. The granite monument is eight feet tall and bears a bronze plate designed by Barry to commemorate the garrison, which stood on this location for a period between 1714 and 1735. This area is now private property. (Author's Collection.)

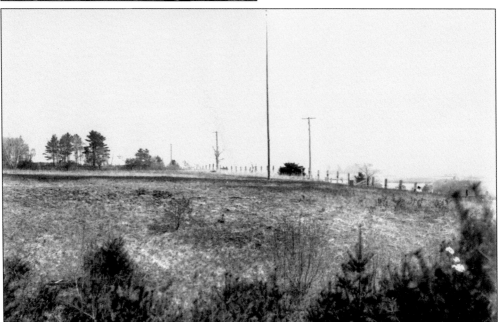

EARLIEST GARRISON MARKER. At the turn of the 20th century, a large flagpole marked the former site of the Larrabee Garrison. Architect and historian William Barry used this marker, deed records, the then-visible graves, and oral tradition to determine the appropriate placement for his granite memorial to the garrison. Local structures still stand nearby, with their provenance validating the location of the garrison. (Glass Negative BSM.)

WILLIAM BARRY, 1846–1932. Architect, artist, and local historian. (84.L.395.)

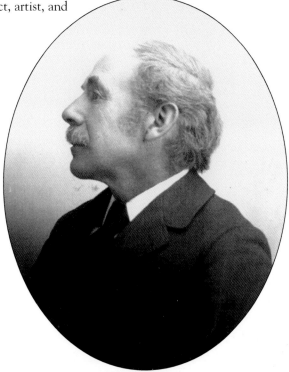

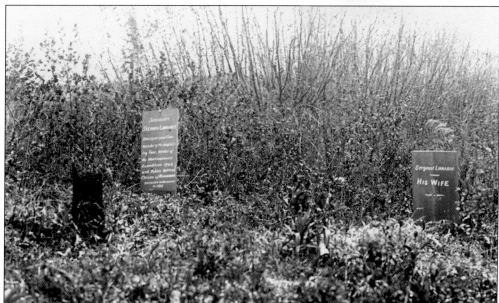

LARRABEE GRAVES. The graves of Larrabee family members lie in close proximity to the garrison site. Unfortunately, over time, the monuments seen in this *c.* 1900 photograph have disappeared. The grave marker on the left reads: "Sergeant Stephen Larrabee, Designer and Commander of the neighboring Fort. Member of the Norridgewock Expedition of 1724 and public spirited citizen of Kennebunk. Deceased subsequent to 1782." The marker on the right reads: "Sergeant Larrabee, His Wife." (Glass Negative BSM.)

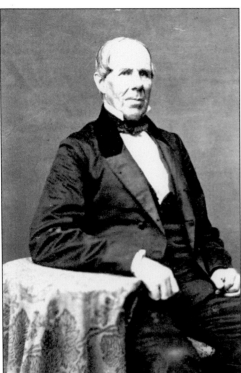

WILLIAM LORD, 1799–1873. Merchant and ship owner. (People File BSM.)

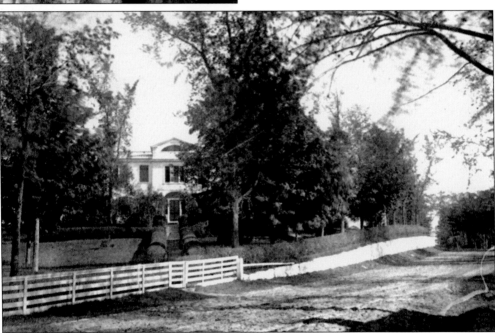

THE WILLIAM LORD MANSION. This is an early stereoview of the home known as the William Lord Mansion. The original ell of this house was built in 1760 by Jonathan Banks, a schoolmaster. The Federal-style front portion of the house that is seen here was built in 1801 by Judge Jonas Clark, who acquired the home in 1789. The house was later purchased by William Lord in 1822. (76.37.4.)

FIRST PARISH UNITARIAN CHURCH.
This ancient New England meetinghouse has been the focal point of Kennebunk since 1772. Originally, the church was smaller, and was called the Second Parish Church of Wells. The structure was enlarged to its present appearance in 1803. The bell was cast by Revere & Son of Boston in 1803. In 1833 the upper galleries of the meetinghouse were floored across to make a lower story for Sunday school classes and social gatherings. Rev. Daniel Little was the first pastor of the church and he served in that role for 50 years. (65.260.)

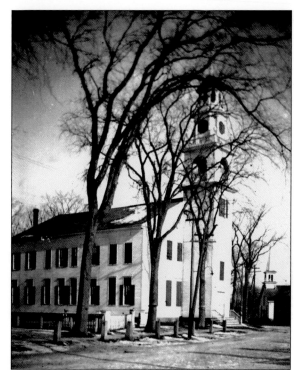

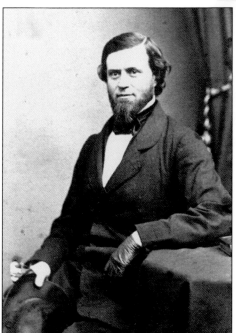
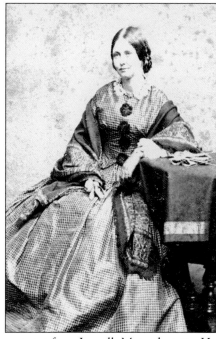

REV. JOSHUA A. SWAN AND HIS WIFE. Reverend Swan came from Lowell, Massachusetts. He was minister of the above church from 1850 until 1869, when ill health forced him to give up his pastorate. He moved to Cambridge, Massachusetts, hoping that a change of location might help restore his health. Unfortunately, his condition did not improve and he died on October 31, 1871. He was succeeded at the Unitarian Church by Rev. Charles Vinal. (People File BSM.)

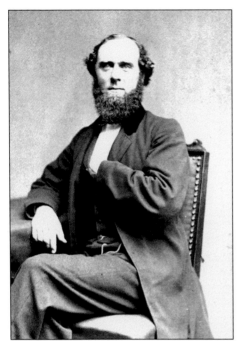 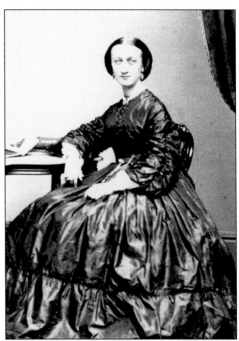

LEFT: HORATIO MOODY, 1826–1887. (People File BSM.) RIGHT: MARY MOODY, 1840–1923. (People File BSM.)

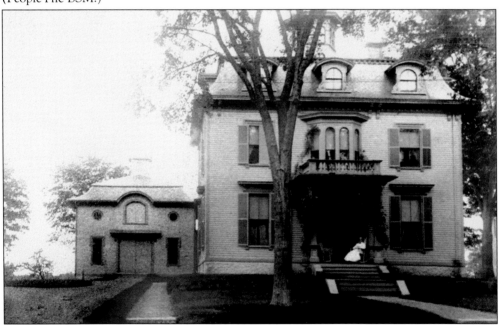

THE HORATIO MOODY HOUSE. This home at 39 Summer Street was built in 1866. On March 10, 1877, Moody and his family sailed from New York, bound for San Francisco. During a storm at sea, while Moody's wife and two sons watched from inside the doorway of the forecastle, a rogue wave stove in the door and washed them out. Mary Moody became caught in the rigging and survived with only broken ribs, but the two boys—George, age 13, and Harry, age 10—were never seen again. News of the accident did not reach Kennebunk until about a month later. (85.L.29.)

14

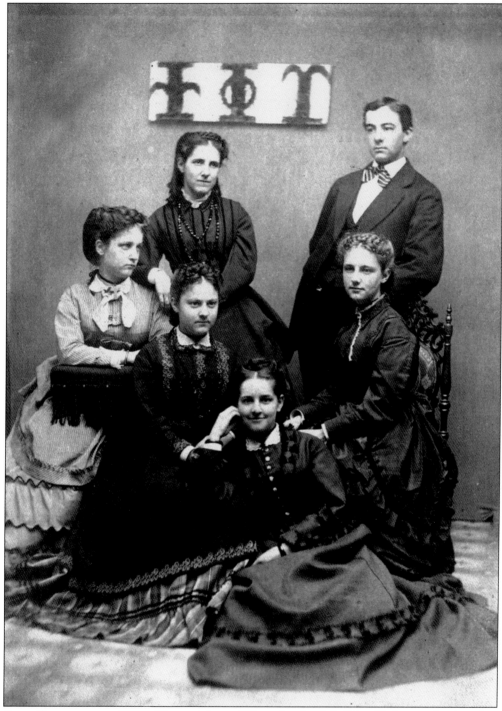

First Graduates of KHS. The members of Kennebunk High School's first graduating class in 1872 are Louisa D. Morton, Ida M. Thompson, Minnie I. Thompson, Susie L. Thompson, William A. Nason, and Annie M. Nason. (1153.1.)

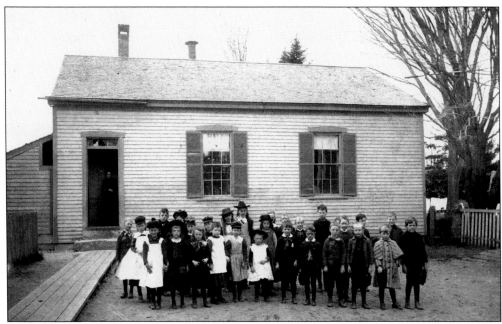

EARLY SCHOOLHOUSE. This small schoolhouse was located behind the Unitarian church. It was built in 1797 and torn down in the early 1930s. (89.34.50.)

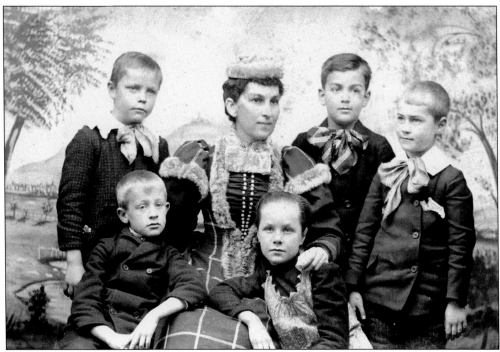

SCHOOL CLASS C. 1892. Students of the early schoolhouse sit for a photograph with their teacher. From left to right are Edgar Harding, Harold Bourne, Annie Allen (teacher), B. Bowen, Arthur Covant, and Cole Arthur. (Private Collection.)

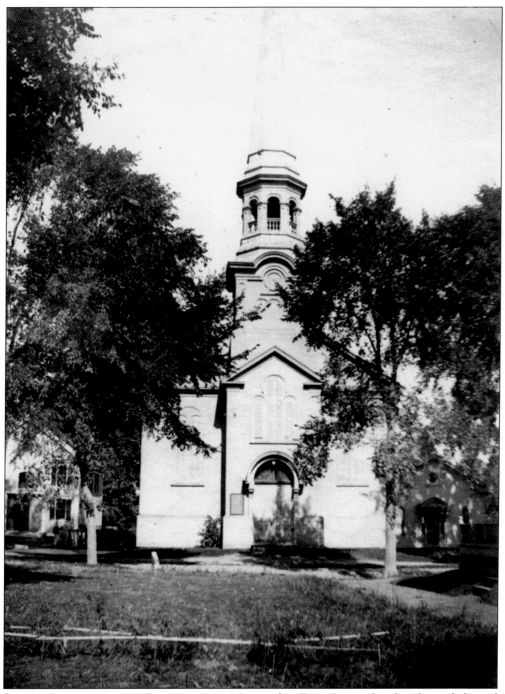

SECOND CONGREGATIONAL CHURCH C. 1900. Located on Dane Street, this church was dedicated on October 7, 1828. It is now called Christ Church. (64.8.258.)

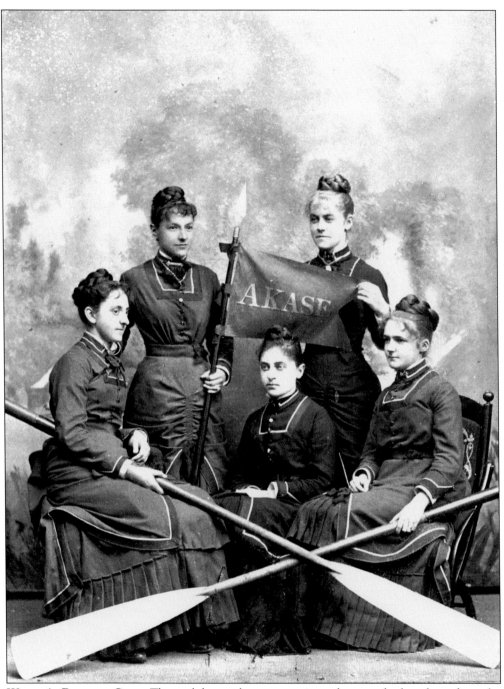

WOMEN'S BOATING CLUB. These club members appear in a photograph that dates from the early 1870s. Pictured are "Kittie" Little (Frost), "Kittie" M. Lord, Addie L. Nason (Loring), Susie L. Maling (Bourne), and Agnes Titcomb (Cole). (1986.)

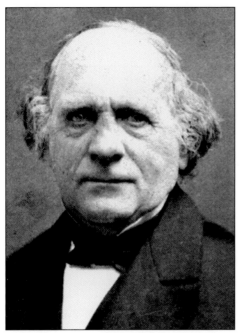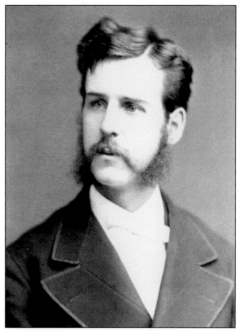

LEFT: DR. ORRIN ROSS. Dr. Ross was born in Kennebunk in 1812. He was a well-respected physician who practiced locally for more than 40 years. Dr. Ross died in June 1881 and is buried at Hope Cemetery. (People File BSM.) RIGHT: DR. FRANK ROSS. The son of Dr. Orrin Ross, Dr. Frank Ross specialized in obstetrics. He never lost a mother during childbirth, and is credited with helping to deliver more than 1,000 babies. In all his years as a town physician, Dr. Ross took but one vacation. He was also active in real estate banking and the Boston and Maine Railroad. (People File BSM.)

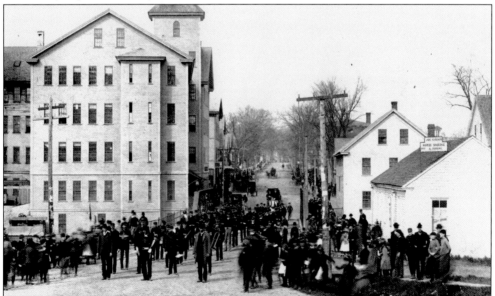

MOUSAM RIVER BRIDGE. In this early photograph of the Mousam River Bridge in Kennebunk, the Davis Shoe factory can be seen on the left side of Main Street. The factory burned down in 1903. (3127.)

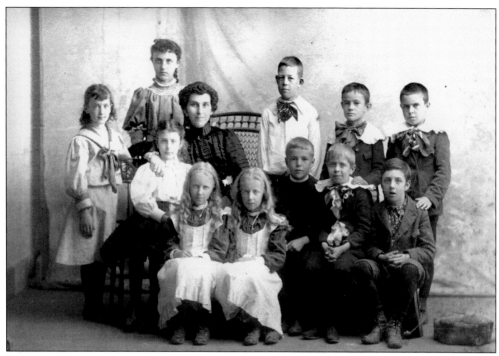

EASTERN PRIMARY SCHOOL CLASS. The school that stood behind the Unitarian church was called the Eastern Primary School. Students of the school are pictured here with their teacher, Annie L. Allen. From left to right are the following: (sitting) Agnes Webb, Miss Allen, Edith and Ethel Furbish, Edward Titcomb, Henry Morton, and George Burgess; (standing) Mary Bourne, Marcia Smith, Ernest Green, Stuart Mendum, and Earl Nedeau. (90.44.17.)

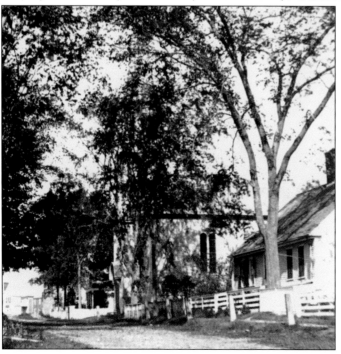

DANE STREET CHURCH AND BUILDINGS. Here is a stereopticon view of Dane Street, looking toward Main Street *c.* 1860. Notice the one-story Cape-style home just before Christ Church. This house originally stood on Ross Road before being moved to this site by Barnabas Palmer. For many years the building served as the parsonage house of the Methodist Society. It has since then been torn down. (2196.1.a.)

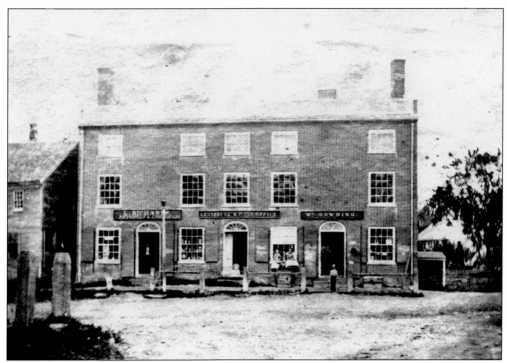

KELLY WARREN BLOCK. The Kelly Warren Block was built about 1818 by Abial Kelly and Alexander Warren. Among the establishments housed there were a grocery store operated by Fred P. Hall, a drugstore originally run by Dr. Lemuel Richards and later by Dr. Bourne, and the post office. On the second floor of the building were tenements, and the entire third floor was originally occupied by the Masonic lodge. The block was moved across the street by Don Chamberlain in 1921 and was used as storage for his automobile business until the structure was finally torn down. (890.)

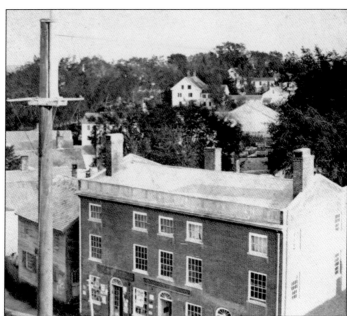

KELLY WARREN BLOCK. This early photograph of the Kelly Warren Block was taken from the steeple of the Unitarian church. (82.34.2y.a.)

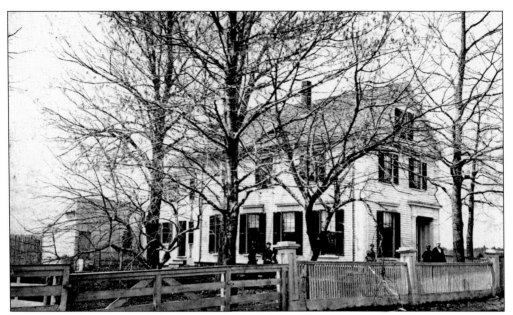

34 STORER STREET. This home was originally built on the eastern corner of Main and Water Streets in 1803, and was relocated to its present site on Storer Street in 1856. Houses were routinely moved by using oxen to pull the structures across greased logs as they were rolled to new locations. (K1053.)

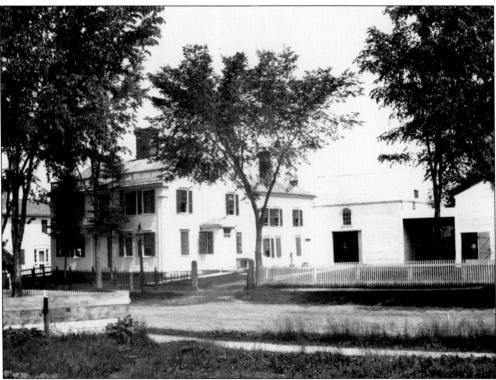

THE TIMOTHY KEZAR HOME. This Fletcher Street home was built for Timothy Kezar in 1806. It is now the Prudential Real Estate office building. (84.L.1109.4.)

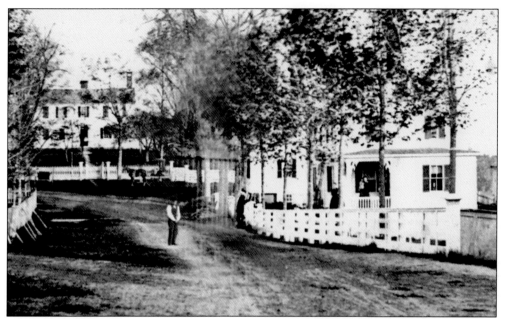

THE CAPT. HENRY FULLER CURTIS HOME. The exact age of this Grove Street house is in question because various documents present different dates for its construction. One source, a 1909 newspaper column commemorating the golden wedding anniversary of Curtis and his wife, said the home was built in 1812 by Henry's father. Other accounts differ. Because the county courthouse kept no official records for when a house was moved, burned down, or was rebuilt, it is hard to know what dates are accurate. (82.34.2r.)

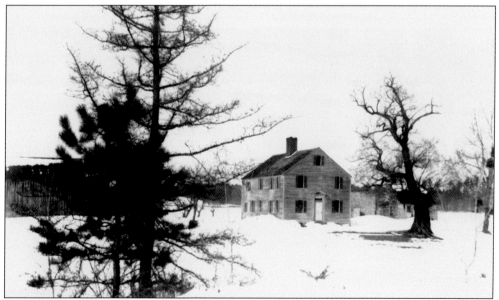

REV. LITTLE'S SECOND HOME. Reverend Little was the first minister of the First Parish Church in Kennebunk. His first house, built at the Landing c. 1752, stands next to the Wedding Cake House. The minister occupied that home until about 1790, when he built another house on upper High Street. This is a vintage photograph of his second home. This residence stood just beyond the home of Joseph Bragdon, and was torn down about 1900. (Private Collection.)

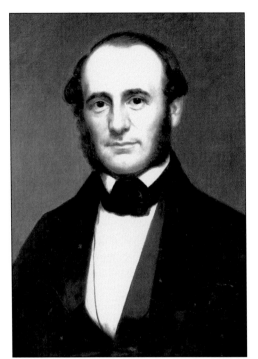
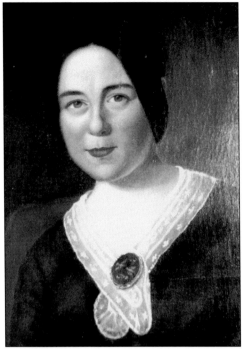

LEFT: CAPT. CHARLES EDWARD BARRY, 1811–1851. This photograph of Captain Barry dates from before 1850. The father of William and Charles Barry, the captain was lost at sea on the ship *William Lord* in 1850. The letters that Captain Barry sent to his wife, Sarah, from his many voyages are part of the Brick Store Museum archives. (88.i.11.) *RIGHT*: SARAH CLEAVES LORD BARRY, 1821–1892. The wife of Capt. Charles Edward Barry. (People File BSM.)

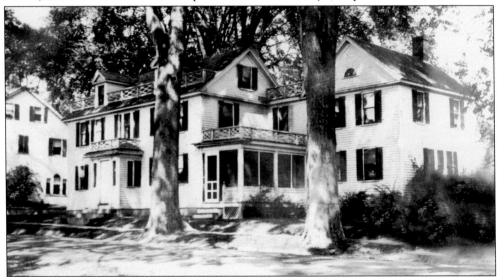

18 DANE STREET. Built about 1815 for Edward Gould, this house later became the first home of Capt. Charles Barry and his wife, Sarah Cleaves. The couple's two sons, William E. Barry and Charles Dummer Barry, were both born here. Following the loss of Captain Barry and the ship *William Lord*, Sarah married Capt. Jott Perkins in 1858 and they moved to a home at 4 Dane Street. (Edith Barry Scrapbook BSM.)

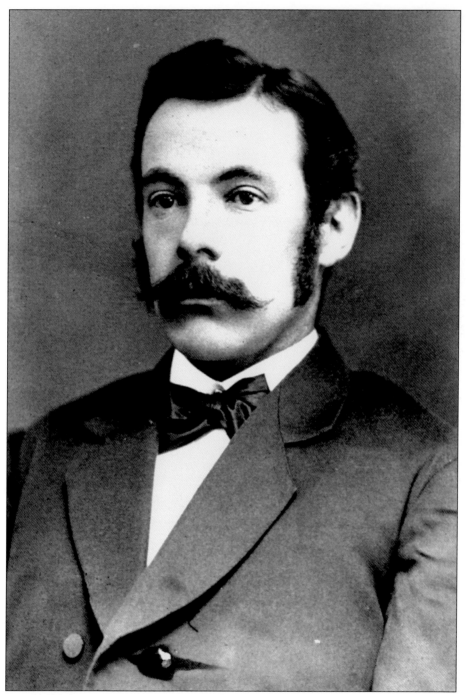

WILLIAM E. BARRY, 1846–1932. Barry was the son of Capt. Charles Barry and Sarah Cleaves. William had a talent for sketching and studied architecture in Europe for two years. After returning to America, he became affiliated with two prominent architectural firms in Boston. William married Florence Wallingford Hooper in 1875. While he is best known as an architect, William Barry was also an ornithologist, preservationist, Sunday school teacher, author, and most importantly, a meticulous town historian. (People File BSM.)

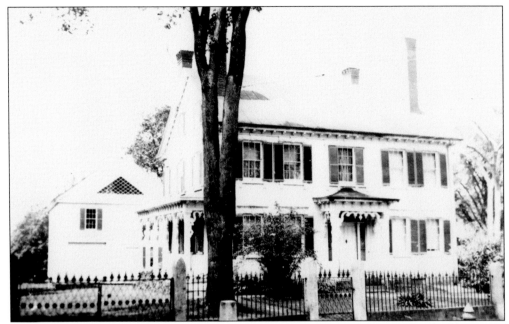

THE BURLEIGH SMART HOUSE. This residence at 21 Summer Street was the first building to be constructed of brick in the village of Kennebunk. The home was erected c. 1825, and remained unpainted until 1852. The barn shown in this photograph (back left) was added by Capt. Franklin N. Thompson, who purchased the house in August 1852 when it went to auction following the death of Mr. Smart. (85.L.10.1.)

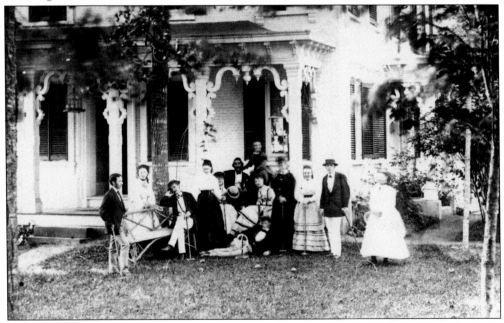

A GENTLE PASTIME. Young croquet players are gathered on the lawn of the Burleigh Smart House at 21 Summer Street. Dr. Smart ran an apothecary shop in the Kelly-Warren block until he relinquished the business to Alexander Warren, who subsequently was succeeded by Dr. Lemuel Richards. (85.L.10.2.)

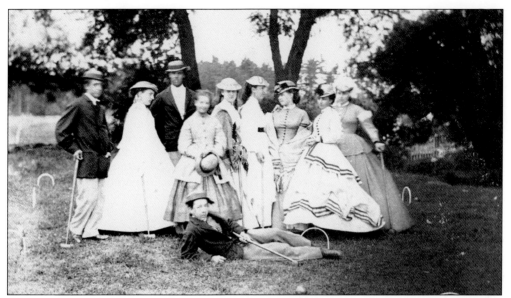

CROQUET PLAYERS. These *c.* 1860 photographs are carte de vista images of a group of young Kennebunk croquet enthusiasts. Identified in the above photograph are Robert W. Nason, Nellie F. Lord, George C. Lord, Annie M. Nason, Charles D. Barry, Mary A. Maling, Lucy A. Thompson, Augusta Nason, Carrie Agery, and Olive Thompson. (1988.3.C.)

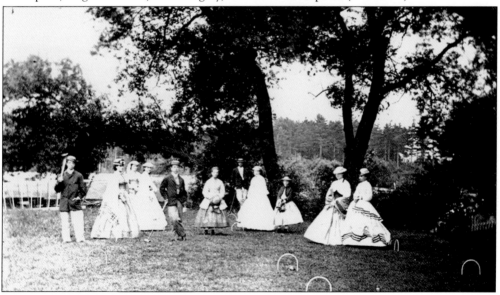

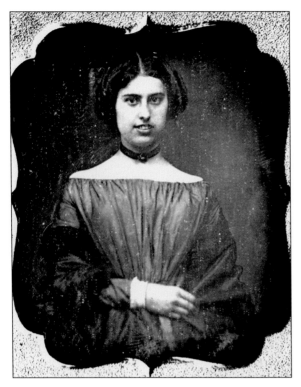

LIZZIE BOURNE. Seen here are two portraits of Lizzie Bourne, the only daughter of Judge Edward Emerson Bourne. On September 14, 1855, when Lizzie was just 23 years old, she and her cousin accompanied her uncle George Bourne (the builder of the Wedding Cake House) on a climb up Mount Washington. They got a late start due to early morning rain on the mountain, and failed to reach the summit by nightfall. As she was weighed down by the yards of fabric of her skirts, pantaloons, petticoats, and stockings—which were common attire of the day—frail Lizzie became exhausted. The darkness closed in, and believing they were far from the summit, the group stopped to rest. At approximately 10 p.m. Lizzie passed away. When daylight came, her companions were horrified to behold the summit only a few hundred yards from where Lizzie had died. (65.401 and 1094.)

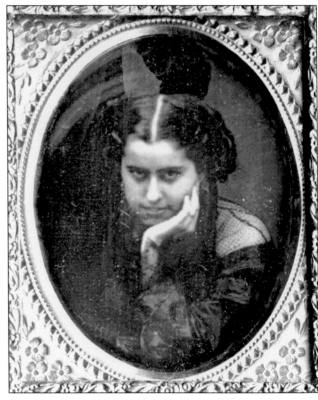

GEORGE BOURNE, BUILDER OF THE
WEDDING CAKE HOUSE. (From
original painting BSM.)

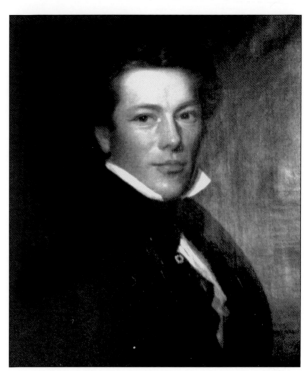

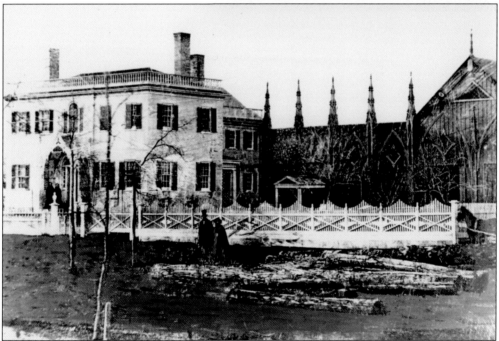

THE GEORGE BOURNE HOUSE. This famous house, now referred to as the Wedding Cake House, was built in 1826. Mr. Bourne designed and carved the wood ornamentations himself, assisted by a ship carpenter's apprentice named Thomas Durrell. The carvings were inspired by cathedrals Bourne had visited in Italy. The name "Wedding Cake House" was fabricated in the early 20th century to attract tourists. (84.1.14.)

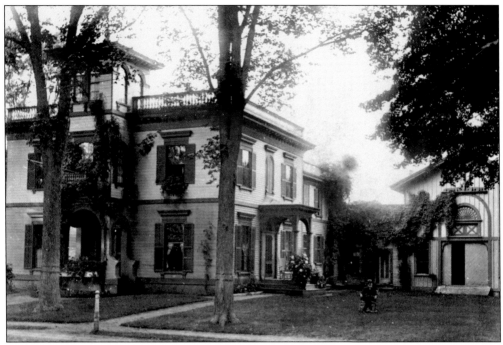

The John Adams Lord House. Located at 32 Summer Street, this home was built in 1855. John Adams Lord was a son of Ivory Lord, who owned a residence located across the street at 31 Summer Street. (85.L.23.1-2.)

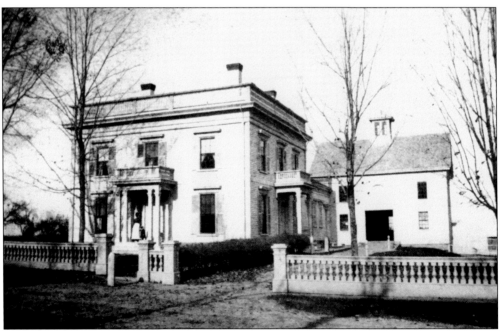

The Moses Maling House. This home at 36 Summer Street was built during the Civil War, in 1862. Maling was a ship captain who sailed to the Orient and collected a vast amount of treasures on his trips. (85.L.28.2.)

Two

CIVIL WAR SOLDIERS

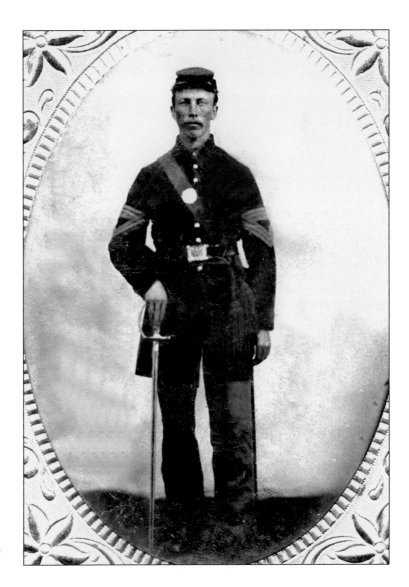

HORACE BURBANK
c. **1864.**(Collection
26 BSM.)

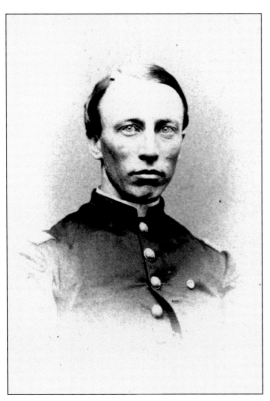

HORACE BURBANK. Burbank's diaries and records are part of the Brick Store Museum collection. Horace Burbank enlisted in the 27th Maine Infantry on August 30, 1862. Although his regiment never fought in a battle, all of its members were (questionably) awarded the Medal of Honor. After his discharge from the military, Burbank went back to school at Bowdoin College and eventually was admitted to the bar. He re-enlisted in the service in 1864 and was mustered in as first lieutenant of Company A, 32nd Maine Volunteers. During the "Battle of the Crater" at Petersburg, Virginia, Burbank was taken prisoner and sent to Andersonville prison, where he remained until his escape in February 1865. Burbank later married the former Lizzie Thompson, daughter of Kennebunk's Capt. Nathaniel Lord Thompson. (People File BSM.)

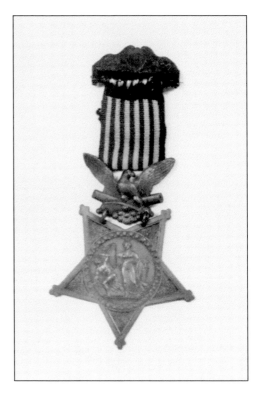

HORACE BURBANK'S MEDAL OF HONOR. (Photograph Courtesy BSM.)

JOHN CLEMENT LORD. The son of Capt. John Lord, John Clement Lord was commissioned ensign in the U.S. Navy on June 22, 1864. He was appointed sailing master on board the steamer *Yantic* and later was appointed navigator on the gunboat *Gettysburg*. Following the Civil War, Lord was a member of the Kennebunk Dramatic Club, which performed many plays at the town hall during the late 1870s. (People File BSM.)

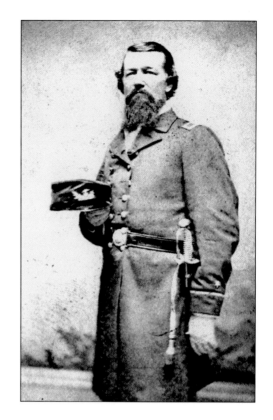

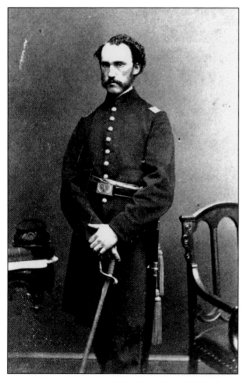

FRANCIS WALLINGFORD SABINE. Francis W. Sabine was the son of Lucretia Wallingford and Francis M. Sabine. The younger Sabine enlisted in the military in November 1861 and served with the 11th Infantry Regiment in the Civil War. He was promoted first to full lieutenant in 1862, then to full captain the same year. On September 17, 1864, Sabine died of wounds suffered in battle. He was a graduate of Bowdoin College and a lawyer by profession. (People File BSM.)

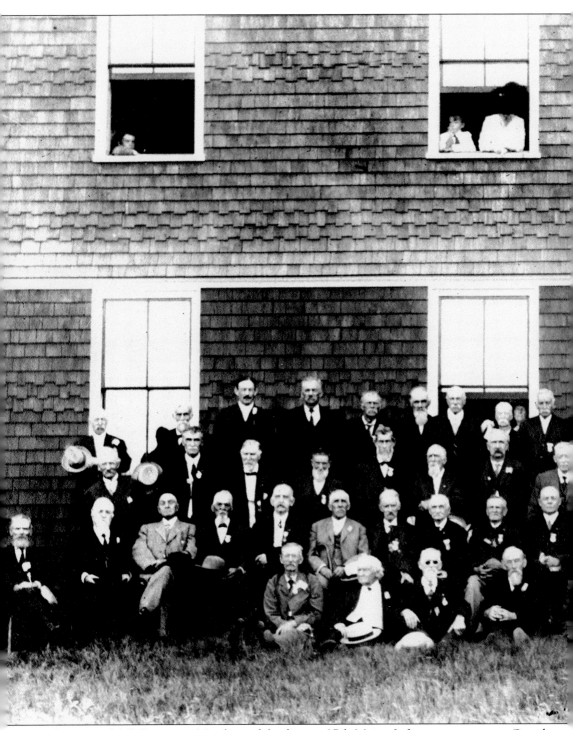

ARUNDEL GAR REUNION. Members of the famous 27th Maine Infantry are seen at a Grand Army of the Republic reunion, which was held at the Arundel Grange hall in 1910. The 27th Maine became the center of a long debate when all of its 864 members were awarded the Medal of Honor due to a bureaucratic mix-up following the Civil War. Only 309

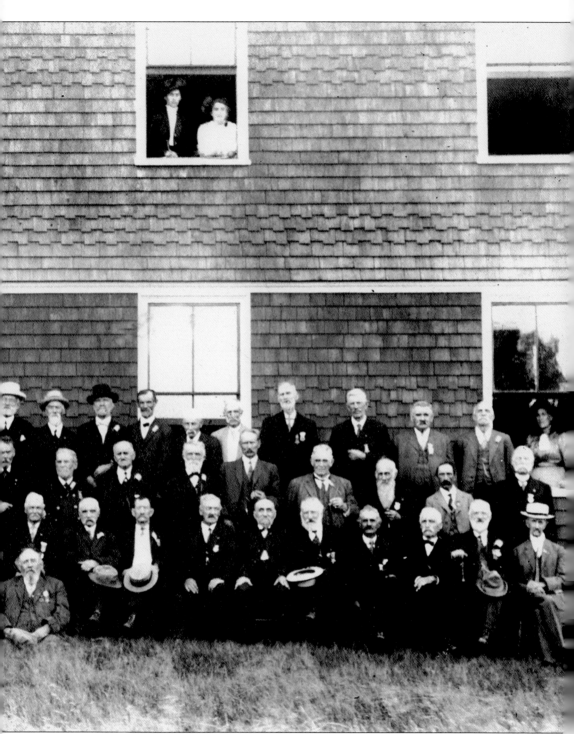

members of the regiment were supposed to have received the medal for extending their service in defense of Washington, D.C., in 1863. In 1916 the federal government tried unsuccessfully to recall the medals. In 1977 Pres. Jimmy Carter officially restored the medals to the regiment. (1993.i.59.)

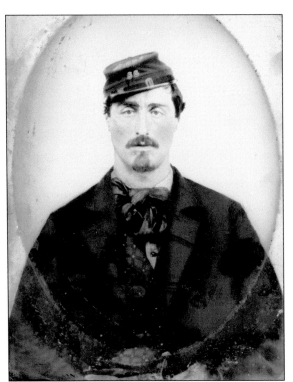

ELBRIDGE HILTON OF WELLS, MAINE. Although he was not from Kennebunk, this Civil War soldier's tintype image is part of the Brick Store Museum's collection. "Elbridge Hilton was 6 feet 2 inches tall in his stocking feet and weighed 206 pounds" according to a man named Thompson, who had shared a tent with him. Hilton died in Andersonville Prison during the war. (64.8.286.)

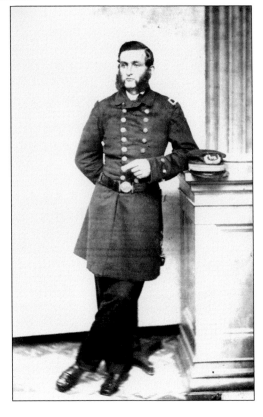

JOSEPH TITCOMB. Born in 1832, Titcomb was originally from Newbury, Massachusetts. He married Francis E. Perkins, who was the daughter of Charles Perkins. In 1861 Titcomb enlisted as a ship master in the Civil War and served for 10 months. Following the war he worked as a coal dealer. (People File BSM.)

SETH BRYANT. Born on March 14, 1826, Seth Bryant enlisted in the 27th Maine Infantry during the Civil War. He served as captain of the infantry's Company I from September 1862 until July 1863. Bryant was awarded the Medal of Honor along with all of his fellow members of the regiment. In March 1864 he again enlisted in the service, and this time was appointed captain of Company A, with the 32nd Maine Infantry. Bryant returned to his Lower Village home after his discharge from the military, and worked as clerk of the Customs House. He died on January 26, 1888. (80.L.88.)

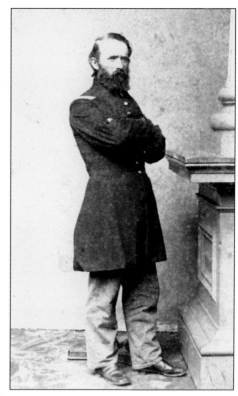

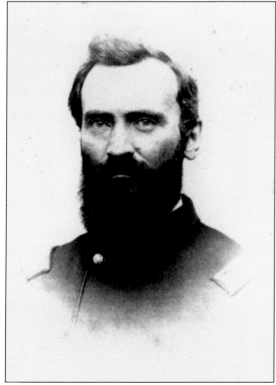

SAMUEL CURTIS SMITH. Samuel was better known as "Curtis" and originally came from Alfred, Maine. He was wounded during his service with the 1st Regiment, Maine Cavalry, at the Battle of Rappahannock in October 1862. He spent his recovery at the home of Henry Fuller Curtis of Kennebunk. Although he never regained full use of his arm, Smith ran a dry goods store in Portland following the Civil War. (People File BSM.)

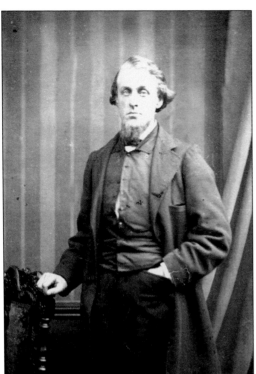

CAPT. WILLIAM SYMONDS. Symonds was commissioned captain in the U.S. Navy in 1864 and served aboard the gunboat *Pinola*. After the war, William, his wife, and their daughter were drowned in a collision of vessels in October 1874. (People File BSM.)

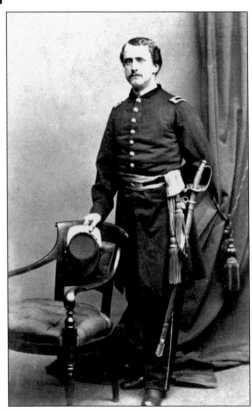

A CIVIL WAR SOLDIER. The identity of this Union Army soldier is not known. (88.31.7.)

Three

In-Town Kennebunk

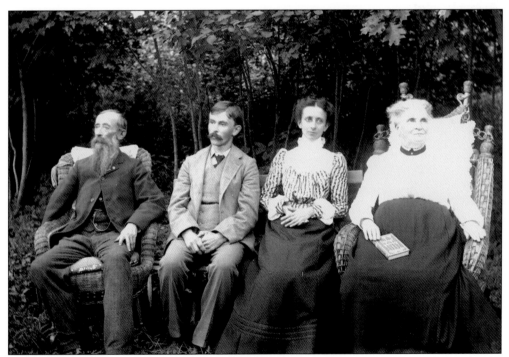

ALBION MOODY FAMILY. Albion Moody, a local photographer, is pictured with his family. From left to right are Albion, son Fred, daughter Lillian, and Albion's wife, Julia. Moody is responsible for many photographic images of Kennebunk taken at the turn of the 20th century. A number of his glass-plate negatives survive and are included in the collections of the Brick Store Museum and the Kennebunk Free Library. Some of his images focus on bizarre subjects, others mundane, but his most important photographs are those of the buildings and homes of Kennebunk. (78M.f.76.)

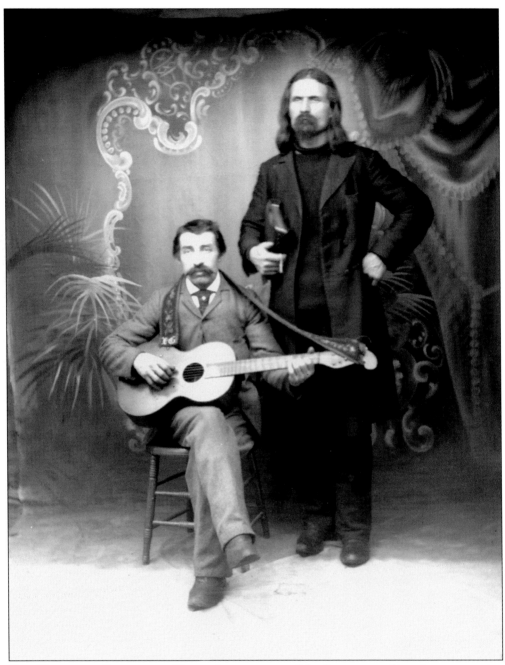

Two Norwegian Immigrants. Norwegians were one of the first groups of immigrants to arrive in Kennebunk. Many of them were encouraged to come to Kennebunk by fellow Norwegian Samuel Tvedt, who is pictured here, standing next to an unidentified guitarist. Samuel and his brother Antoine arrived from Bergen, Norway, in the late 1880s. Antoine was employed making roving cans at the Leatheroid factory on Water Street. Samuel held a variety of jobs through the years, but is best remembered as a flamboyant preacher of the Gospel. It was said that, on a regular basis, Sam would stand at the village pump while waving his Bible and proclaiming the Gospel, at the top of his lungs, to anyone and no one. (78M.m.5.)

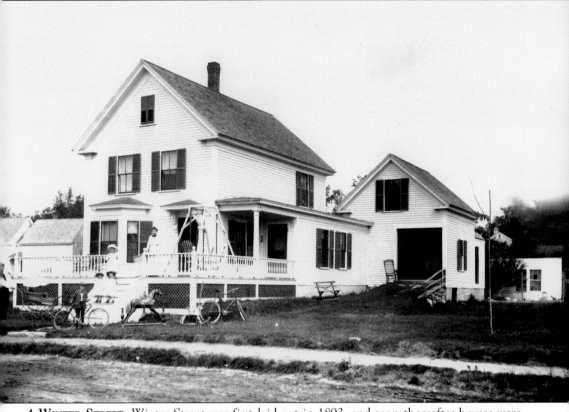

4 WINTER STREET. Winter Street was first laid out in 1893, and soon thereafter houses were built along this convenient route to the depot. This home was constructed that same year by immigrant Antoine Tvedt, who worked for the Leatheroid Company. Tvedt and his family posed in front of the house for this photograph in 1894. (78M.p.28.)

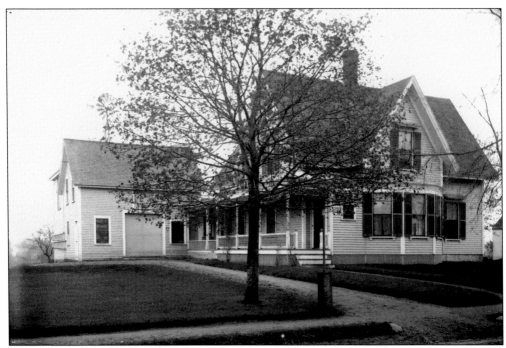

30 Park Street. This Moody photograph was taken c. 1900. Park Street was laid out from Summer Street to Dane Street about 1815, and then was extended to Grove Street in 1884. This home at 30 Park Street was built for Hattie E. Fairfield in the fall of 1884. (78M.p.8.)

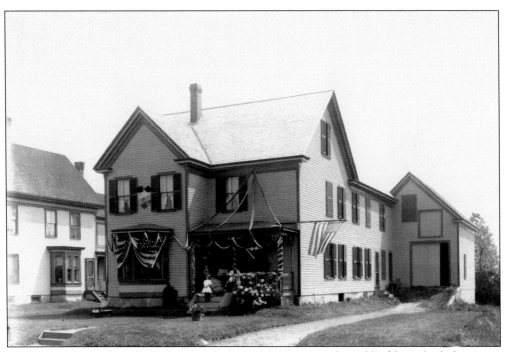

36 Park Street. The Albert Keene Home stood at No. 36 Park, and had been built for Keene in the fall of 1884. This photograph was taken around the turn of the 20th century. (78M.p.9.)

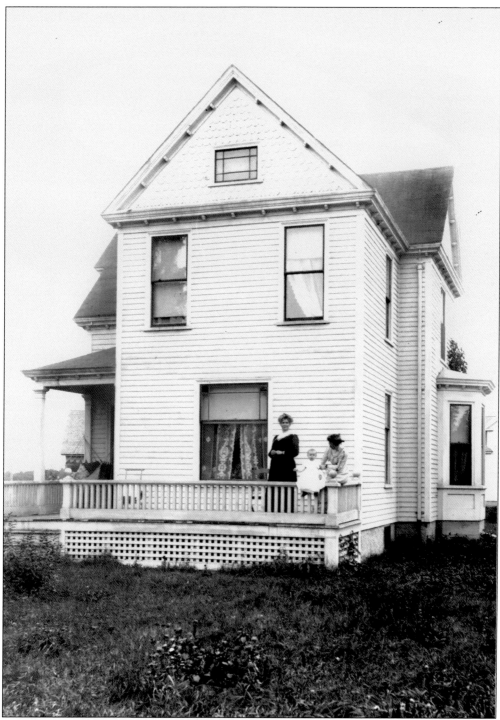

THE GETCHELL HOME. Many will not recognize this house, since it has been modified over the years to accommodate various business ventures. Located at the corner of York and Day Streets, the building was most recently occupied by the Square Toes Restaurant. The original residence was built *c.* 1880 for the Getchell family. (78M.p.5.)

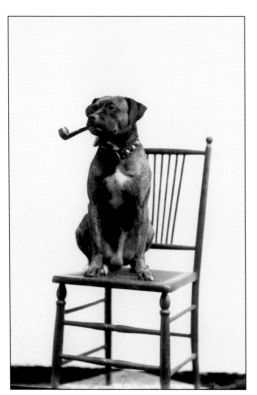

A Clever Dog and His Pipe. An Albion Moody photograph. (78M.n.22.)

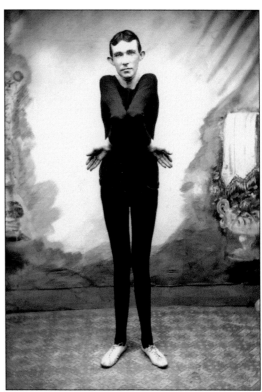

An Amazing Contortionist. Photographed by Albion Moody, the name of this gentleman is unknown. (78M.j.388.)

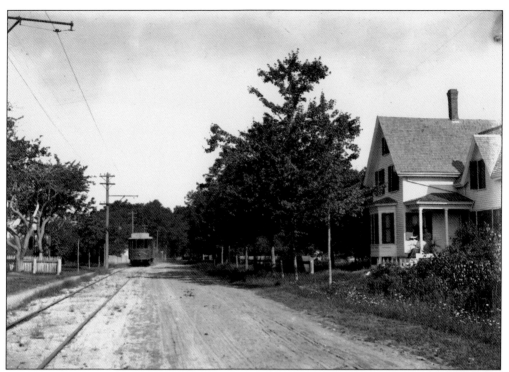

FLETCHER STREET SCENE. A trolley travels along Fletcher Street in this view. The house on the right was the home of photographer Albion Moody and family at 47 Fletcher Street. Moody's wife and daughter can be seen seated on the porch. (85.12.5.36.b.)

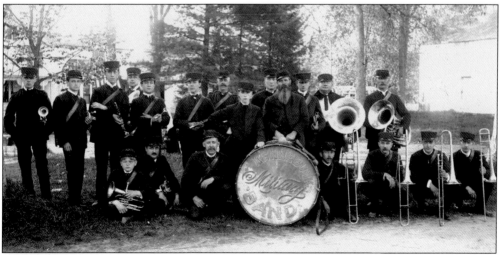

THE KENNEBUNK MILITARY BAND. This band was a very busy group in the 1870s and 1880s. These musicians played at most of the major functions in town, ranging from parades to benefits. (85.i.46.)

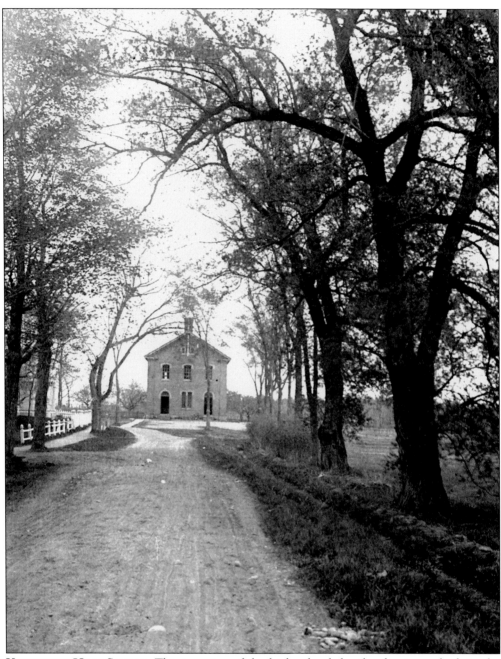

KENNEBUNK HIGH SCHOOL. This is a view of the high school shortly after it was built in the early 1870s. At the time this photograph was taken, Park Street had not yet been laid out from Dane Street to Grove Street. (Photo Album 2871.)

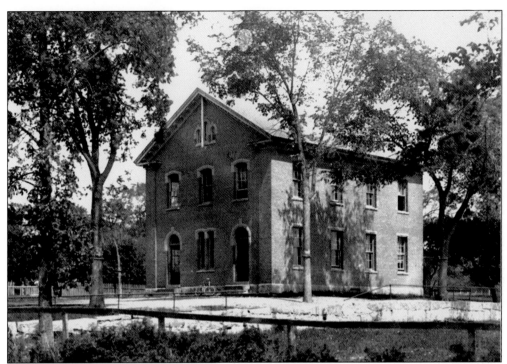

KENNEBUNK HIGH AND GRAMMAR SCHOOL. The first school to be built on the site of the present-day Park Street School was called Union Academy. Constructed in 1833, it was a private school funded by subscription. It burned down on April 18, 1870, and arson was suspected as the cause. The next school to be built on the site was the two-story brick structure seen here, which was known as Kennebunk High and Grammar School. (2356.)

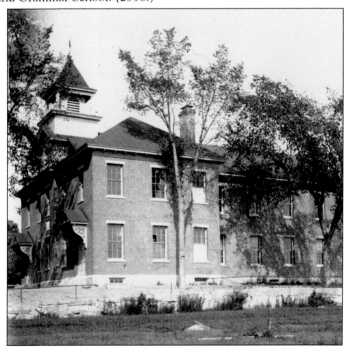

THE 1898 ADDITION. The high school building was enlarged in 1898. This view shows the front of the building and the two-story section that was added. This structure was torn down in 1920 to make way for the present school building. (2357.)

47

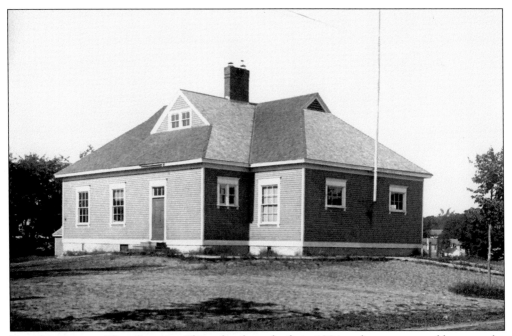

THE CENTENNIAL HILL SCHOOL. This school was built in 1884 and was so named because the land on which it stood was originally a field used during the Centennial celebration. (BSM Photo album 2871.)

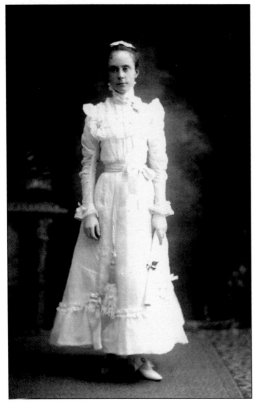

MISS GERTRUDE YOUNG. Miss Young is shown here in a portrait taken after her graduation from Kennebunkport High School in 1900. Years later she became a teacher at the Centennial Hill School. As an adult Gertrude lived on Winter Street in the home built by Antoine Tvedt. (Kennebunk Alumni Association.)

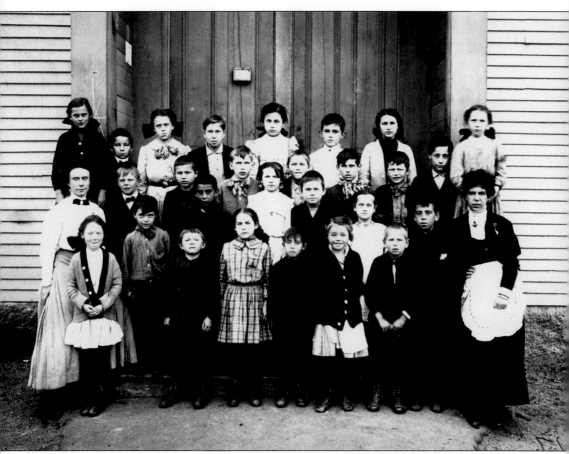

CENTENNIAL HILL STUDENTS WITH MISS YOUNG. Students at the Centennial Hill School pose for a class picture with teachers Gertrude Young (far left) and Mabel Kelley (far right). Although not all of these pupils are identified, the class members who are listed include Emily Waterhouse, Raymond Whicher, Eva Austin, Maurice Stevens, Marcie Frechette, Irvin Noble, Lizzie Charette, Maggie Octeau, Alfred Spiller, George Frechette, Earle Waterhouse, Joe Stevens, Dana Charette, Dana Adams, Arthur Beaudoin, Victor Bernier, Alfred Frechette, Blanche Paradis, Neva Webber, Charlie Adams, Jesse Junkins, Bernice Nason, Norman Knight, Ruby Spiller, Fred Stevens, and Eugene Bernier. (Private Collection.)

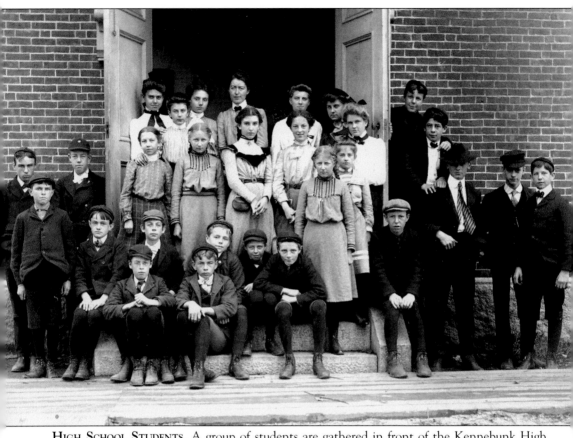

HIGH SCHOOL STUDENTS. A group of students are gathered in front of the Kennebunk High School when it was located on Park Street. (90.44.18.)

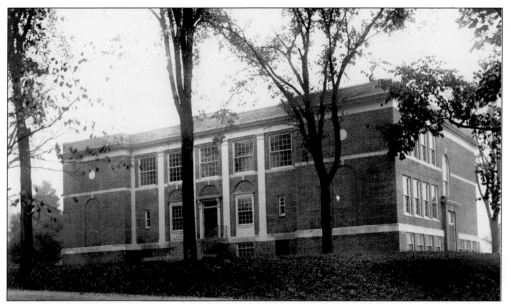

PARK STREET SCHOOL. The present building on this site was erected in 1921 as a high school. Currently an elementary school, it is scheduled to close in 2004. A new school has been built in West Kennebunk. (Private Collection.)

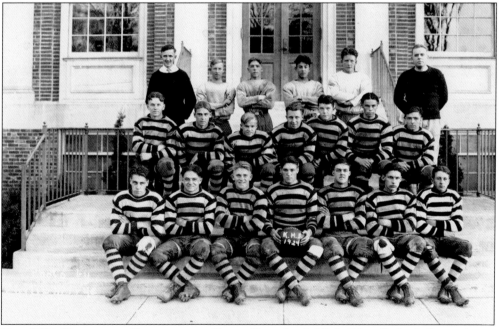

THE 1924 KENNEBUNK CHAMPIONSHIP TEAM. Kennebunk High School's football squad won the York County championship in 1924. Team members are, from left to right, as follows: (first row) John Eckert Jr., Alfred Smith, Harold York, Millett Day, Charles Cousens, Elfred Leech, and Norman Perkins (second row) Roland Webber, Raymond ("Bobby") Coombs, Rodney Kelley, Carleton Miner, Carleton Hayes, Byron Day, and Charles Wormwood; (third row) Roger Furbish, Dauson Savage, Elwyn Lahar, Maurice Baitler, Leonard Lombard, and Coach Arthur Mulraney. (90.3.1.)

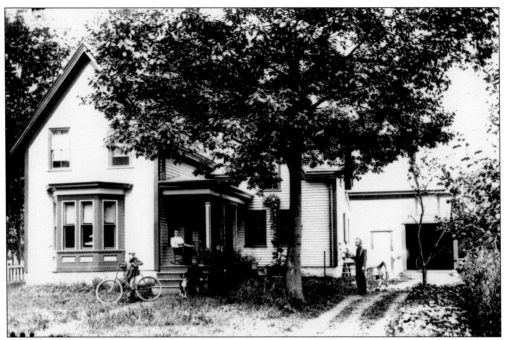

FAMILY AT 51 FLETCHER STREET C. 1900. (78M.p.27.) In this era it was customary for families to pose with horses, oxen, family heirlooms, or even bicycles to convey a sense of wealth.

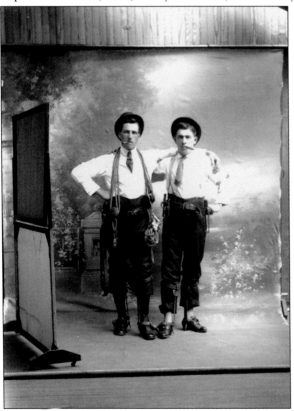

POSING FOR THE CAMERA. It is unclear what these two men did for a living. Moody's studio curtains and screens can be seen in the photograph. Perhaps these men climbed steeples or other high buildings. (78M.h.80.)

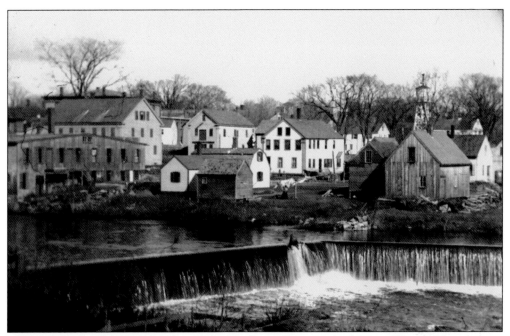

MOUSAM RIVER VIEW. Pictured is the Lower River Dam on the Mousam River. This dam no longer exists. Also visible is the small gambrel-roofed house that is still located at 7 Water Street. The house dates from the 1700s. (2000.52.4.)

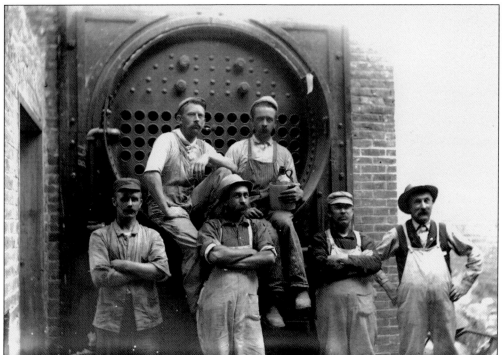

CANDID SHOT. Everyday workmen were also the subjects of Albion Moody's camera. This unidentified group shares a pose with their jug at one of the factories that operated on the banks of the Mousam River. (78M.h.72.)

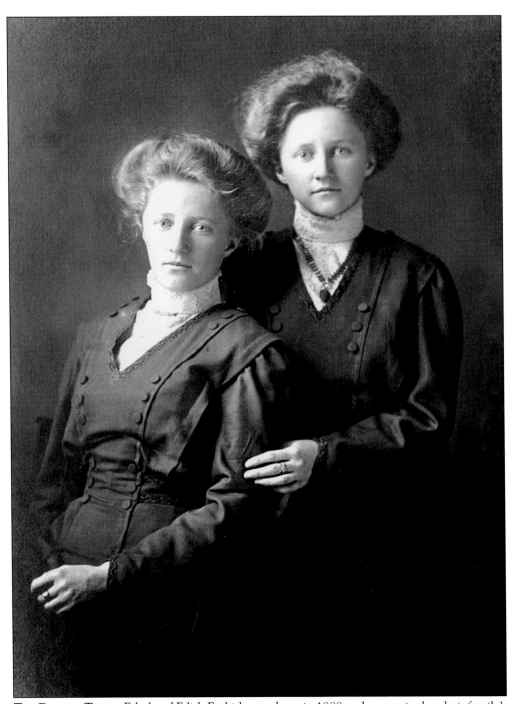

THE FURBISH TWINS. Ethel and Edith Furbish were born in 1888 and were raised at their family's farm at 14 Sea Road. They both attended Kennebunk schools, and although each was engaged to be wed at one point, neither did marry. The sisters lived together at the Sea Road homestead until their later years, then finally moved into the Saco River Health Center in Biddeford, where they lived out the remainder of their lives. Edith, who was born five minutes before Ethel, outlived her sister. (People File BSM.)

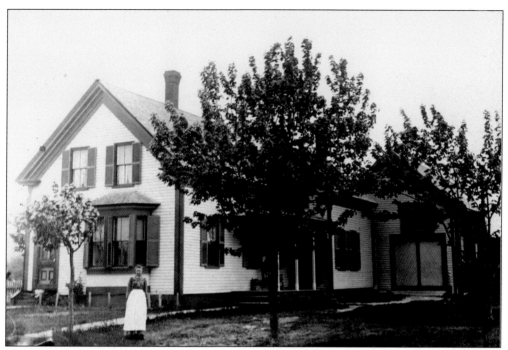

THE GEORGE FURBISH HOME. The house at 14 Sea Road is where the Furbish twins, Edith and Ethel, were born. (90.44.74.)

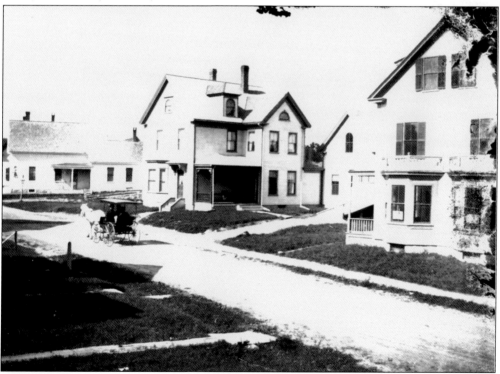

GROVE STREET SCENE. Seen here is a vintage view of a carriage on Grove Street *c.* 1900. (Glass Negative BSM.)

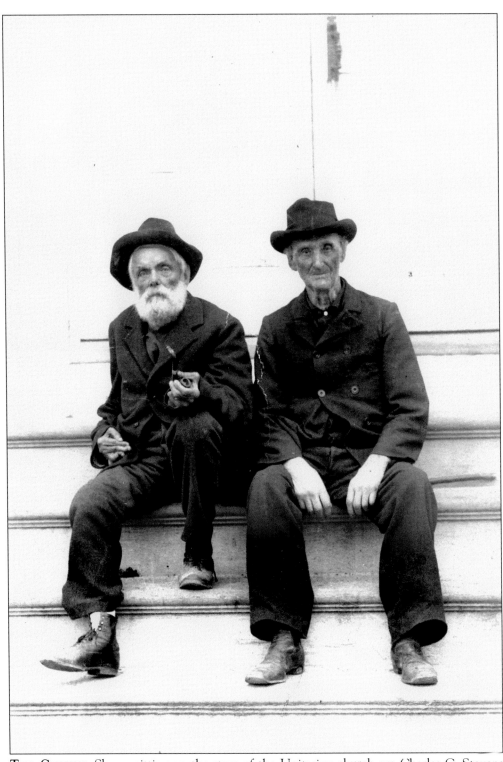

Two Citizens. Shown sitting on the steps of the Unitarian church are Charles C. Stevens (left), a jeweler by trade, and Eben Huff, sexton of the church. (90.16.)

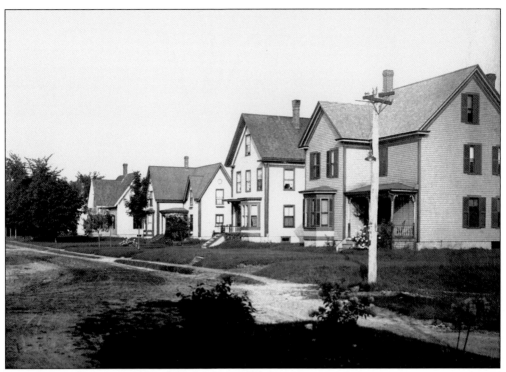

Park Street Scene c. 1900. (BSM Album 2871.)

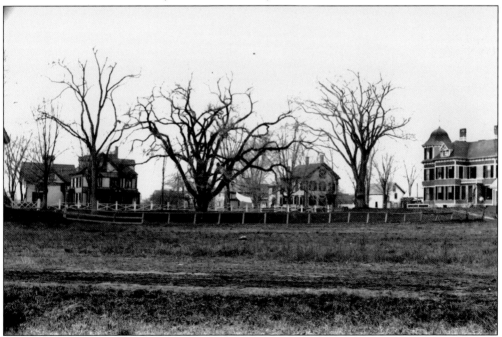

Lafayette Elm. This image shows the famous Lafayette elm tree that stood in the field beside the Storer Mansion. This elm reportedly provided shade for General Lafayette when he delivered a speech in Kennebunk in 1825. The elm succumbed to Dutch elm disease and was cut down in 1971. A cross section of this tree has been saved at the Brick Store Museum. (Glass negative 74.)

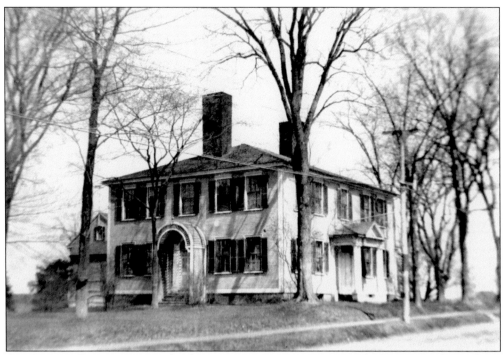

THE TAYLOR-BARRY HOUSE. This home at 24 Summer Street was built in 1803 for William Taylor by Thomas Eaton, a well-known architect of his day. In 1818 the residence was sold at auction by Taylor and came into the possession of Charles Williams. (90.74.4.)

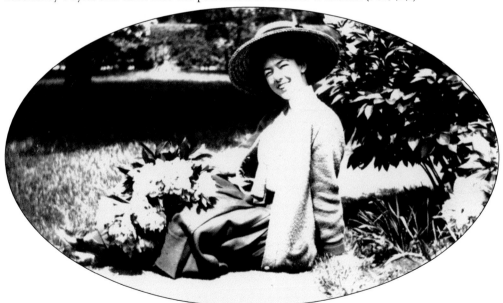

EDITH CLEAVES BARRY. The Taylor-Barry House took its name in part from Edith Cleaves Barry, who lived in the home during her summers in Kennebunk. Barry was the founder of the Brick Store Museum and was a great-granddaughter of Capt. William Lord. The house contains fine samples of stencils executed by itinerant artist Moses Eaton Jr. of Hancock, N.H. (People File BSM.)

58

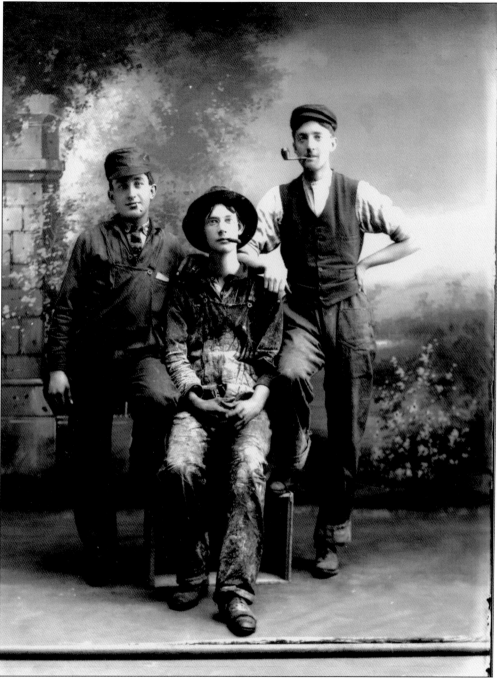

WORKERS AT REST. Three unidentified tradesmen are captured in a pose at Albion Moody's photography studio, which stood on the corner of Brown Street in the 1890s. (78M.h.81.)

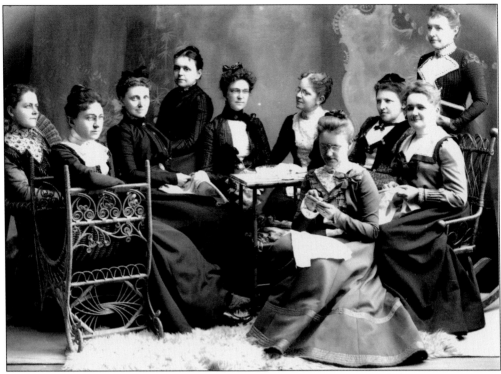

THE WEDNESDAY CLUB. These ladies of the First Parish Church met regularly for many years to sew. They made clothing for the poor and raised money for the improvement of the Centennial plot, at the northern end of Main Street in front of the church. Here posing are, from left to right, Susan Maling Bourne, Agnes Titcomb, Lizzie Tucker, Maria Stone Titcomb, Helen Lord Brigham, Lucy A. Thompson, Frances Hastings Goodnow, Nellie Parsons, Kate Lord, and Elizabeth Frost. (78M.g.113.a.)

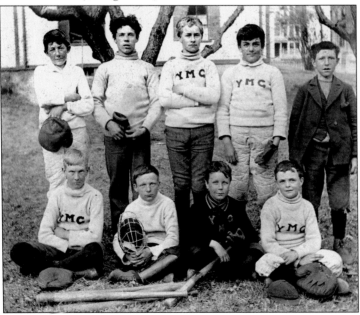

KENNEBUNK BASEBALL TEAM. This picture was taken near the Centennial Hill School on Grove Street. Although not all of the boys are identified, included in this group are Burt Furbish, Arthur Cole, Arthur Conent, George Phillips, C. Knight, Chris Christensen, Roy Nason, and George Ward. (84.L.29.)

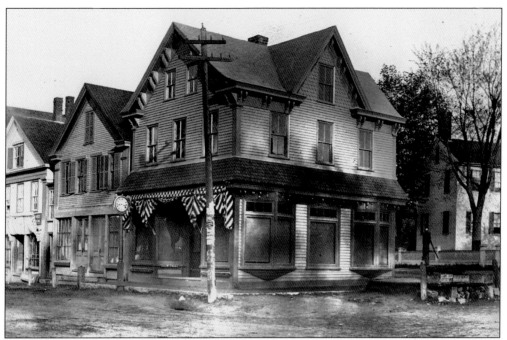

MAIN STREET VIEW. Here is a rare view of the old town pump on Main Street. The wooden building in the center of the photograph was built in the early 1800s by Capt. John Low. Decades later, Frank Barrett operated his jewelry store here, until the building burned down in in 1923. The brick building that replaced this structure is the current home of the Kennebunk Toy Company. On the right can be seen a rare glimpse of the Dr. Orrin Ross Home, which once stood on the site of the present-day parking lot for Garden Street Market. (84.L.26.)

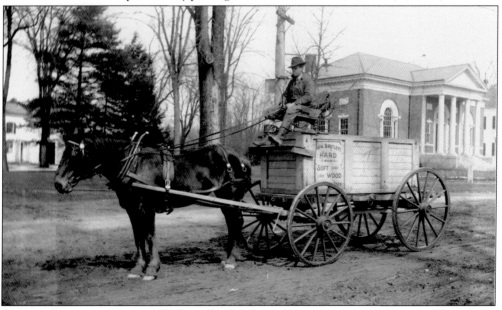

WILLIAM BARTLETT WAGON. William Bartlett began operating a saw mill on the Kennebunk River in the early years of the Civil War. This vehicle was used to transport wood to his customers. (85.12.5.45.)

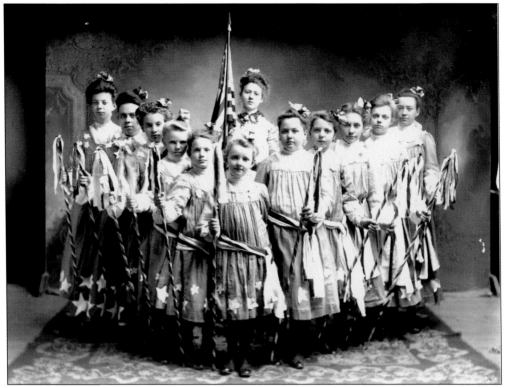

Rainbow Girls. This image of the "Rainbow Girls" was taken at the turn of the 20th century. It is not clear if the group was affiliated with the Masonic youth organization of the same name. (1995-15.)

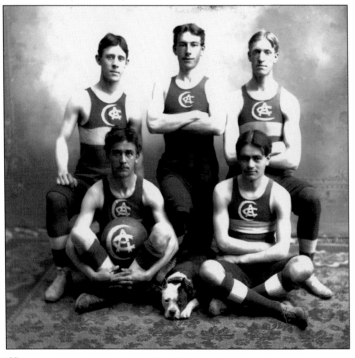

Basketball Squad. Teammates Willis Watson, George Fiske, Ira Wells, Charles Hatch, and Henry McBride pause for a photo shoot. (89.i.26.)

TWO TRADESMEN. An unidentified painter and ice delivery man pose with the tools of their trade in the studio of Albion Moody. (78M.h.82.)

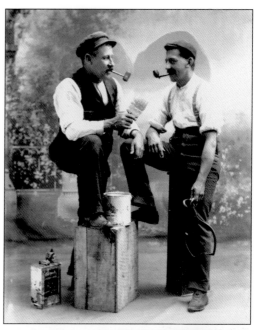

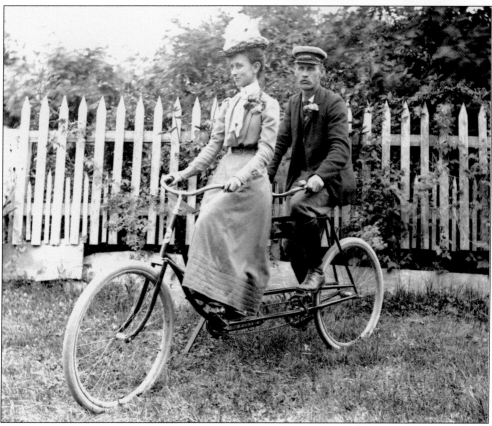

A BICYCLE BUILT FOR TWO. Lillian Moody, daughter of Albion Moody, rides tandem with an unidentified gentleman c. 1905. (78M.f.73.)

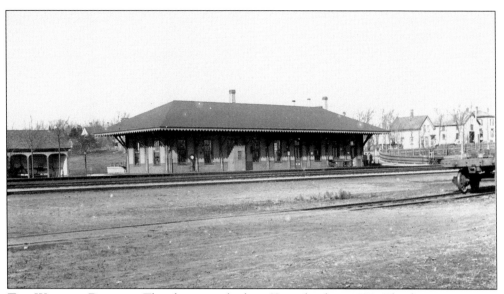

THE WESTERN DIVISION. This depot was built in Kennebunk in 1872. The first train to pass through this section, known as the Western Division, ran on March 27, 1873. (84.L.271.C.)

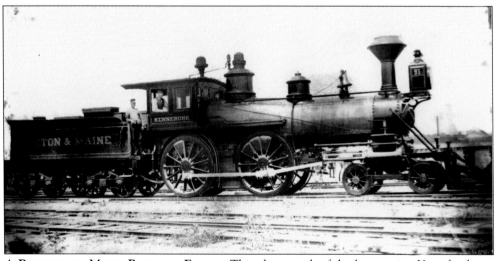

A BOSTON AND MAINE RAILROAD ENGINE. This photograph of the locomotive *Kennebunk* was taken in 1883. (84.L.276.)

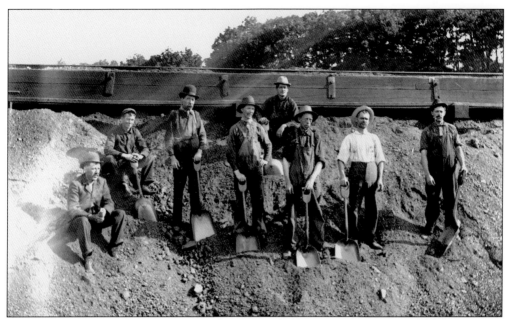

RAILROAD WORKERS. This crew of workmen, photographed by Albion Moody, are busy at work on a railroad embankment. (78M.h.84.)

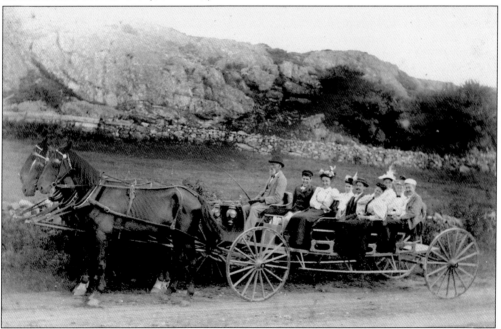

WOODBURY HALL'S COACH SERVICE. Mr. Woodbury Hall came to Kennebunk from Shapleigh, Maine, and for a time, he owned and operated the Mousam House on Tavern Hill.

Hall also operated a coach service for travelers between the railroad depots—he is at the reins of the coach seen here. Hall lived on Main Street in the Pomfret Howard House, which was built in 1788. He housed a few select boarders at his home and carried on a livery stable there. Eventually the house was torn down to make way for a gas station. It is said that Woodbury Hall was a horseman all his life and a thoroughly honest one. He died in 1922. (People File BSM.)

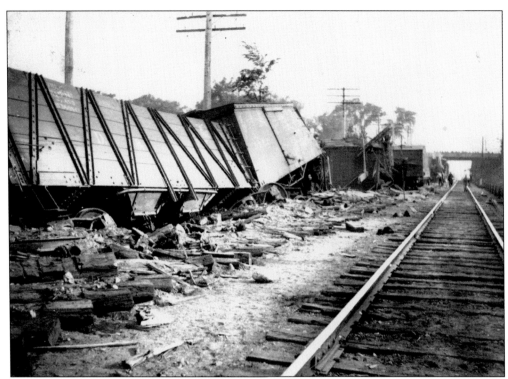

TRAIN WRECK IN KENNEBUNK. These images were captured at the scene of the September train wreck of 1914. A train carrying 1,000 tons of coal jumped the tracks just below the Summer Street Bridge. Luckily, no one was injured. (Private Collection.)

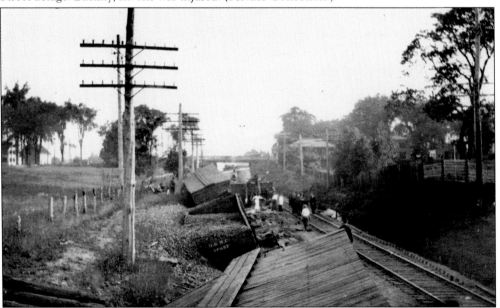

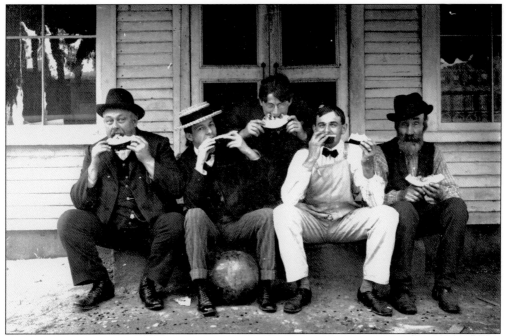

WATERMELON ON A HOT SUMMER DAY. Many of Albion Moody's striking images leave us wondering who these individuals were that posed for him. If Moody did keep a record of the people he photographed, it has never been found. (78M.h.65.)

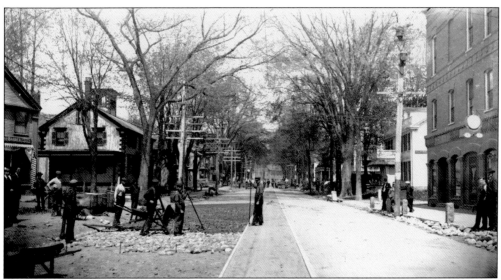

MAIN STREET ROADWORK. This image by Albion Moody shows a group of men putting crushed stone between the rails of the trolley tracks on Main Street in November 1899. The home on the left was built in 1808 for Capt. Charles Perkins, and in 1912 the structure was raised up so that the Bowdoin drugstore could be built underneath it. This building was demolished in 1999. (85.L.51.c.)

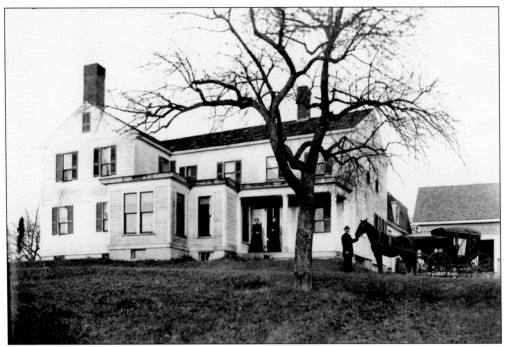

THE HENRY F. CURTIS HOME ON GROVE STREET C. 1905. Henry Curtis, a Civil War veteran, is seen standing in front of the carriage on the right, holding his horse's reins. (The women on the front porch are not identified.) Curtis's home had been completely renovated by William Barry c. 1890. (Glass negative BSM.)

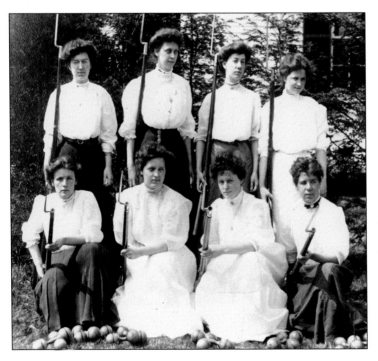

KENNEBUNK PYTHIAN SISTERHOOD C. 1910. This group of ladies, an auxiliary branch of the Knights of Pythias, held ceremonial rifle drills, calisthenics competition, and Indian club drills. (84.L.281.)

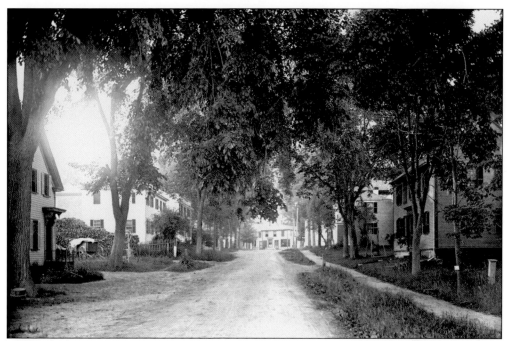

FLETCHER STREET SCENE. This is a view of Fletcher Street, looking toward Main Street. The picture was reproduced from a glass negative of a photograph taken around 1905. The houses on the right are no longer standing. (Glass negative 308.)

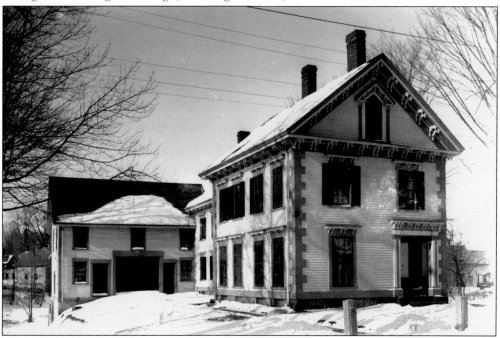

THE CHARLES DRESSER HOME AT 10 STORER STREET. Dresser built this home in 1853, and a drawing of the house appeared on the well-known 1856 Map of York County. Charles Dresser was born in Kennebunk in 1826. In 1844 he opened a grocery store on Main Street and sold furniture and men's clothing. He died in 1906. (Glass negative 100.)

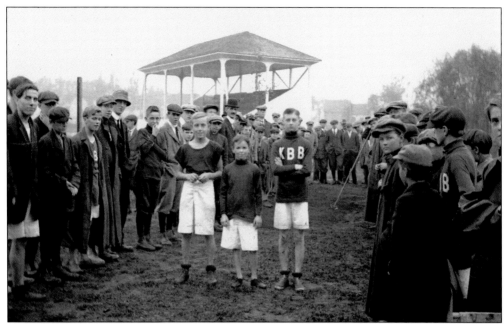

PARK STREET GRANDSTAND. The grandstand, built in 1911, can be seen in the background of this photograph taken during what appears to be a track meet *c.* 1915. (Private Collection.)

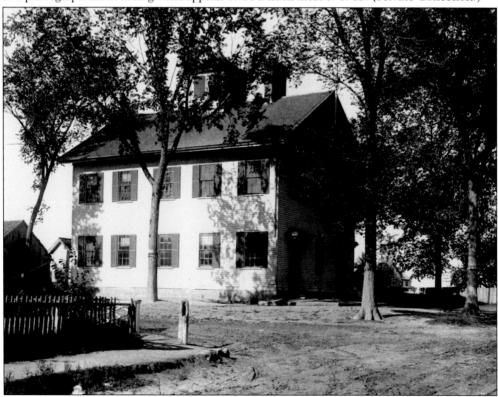

SWAN STREET SCHOOL. This school was built in 1856 and was closed in 1936 after Cousens School was constructed on Day Street. (BSM Photo Album 2871.)

THE FIREHOUSE ON FLETCHER STREET. This firehouse was built on Fletcher Street in the late 1880s. Unfortunately the station fell victim to "progress" in the 1960s and was torn down to make room for a bank parking lot. (84.L.23.)

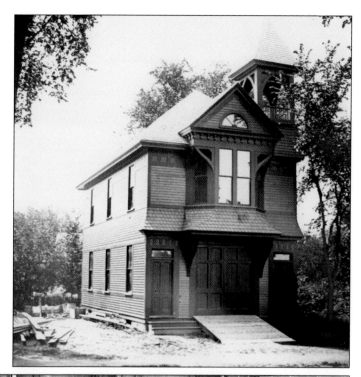

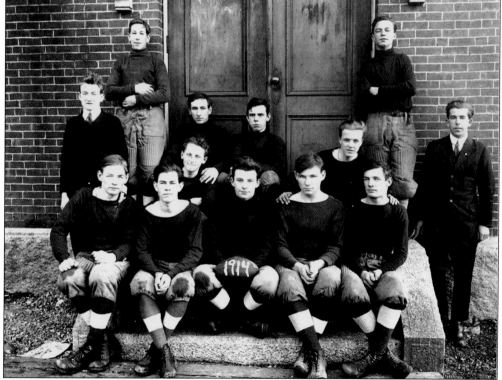

KENNEBUNK FOOTBALL TEAM. While we do know that these lads played football together in 1914, their names are not known. (89.34.52.a.)

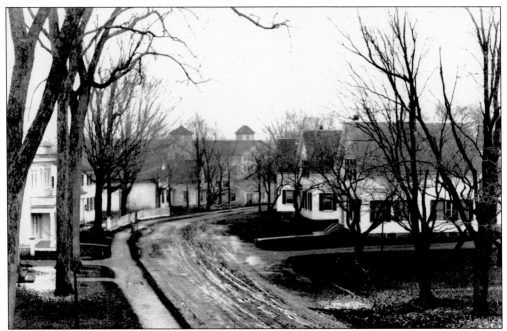

PLEASANT STREET PROSPECT. A view of the Pleasant Street neighborhood, looking toward town *c.* 1900. (Glass negative BSM.)

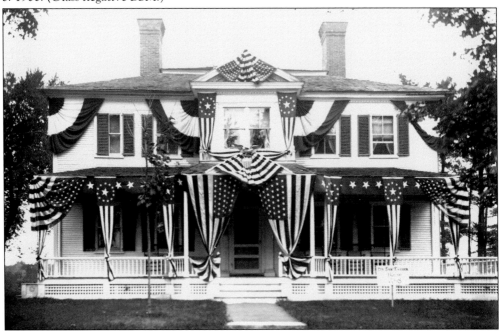

THE SAMUEL EMERSON HOUSE. Located at 35 Pleasant Street, this home was built between 1797 and 1798. Samuel Emerson was a physician, born in Hollis, New Hampshire. At the age of 11, Emerson was a fifer in the Revolutionary War. He received his medical education at Harvard, and settled in Kennebunk in 1790. Somewhere in the fields and meadows surrounding this farm is the grave of Revolutionary War soldier Maj. Nathaniel Cousens; information about its exact location has been long lost. (Glass Negative BSM.)

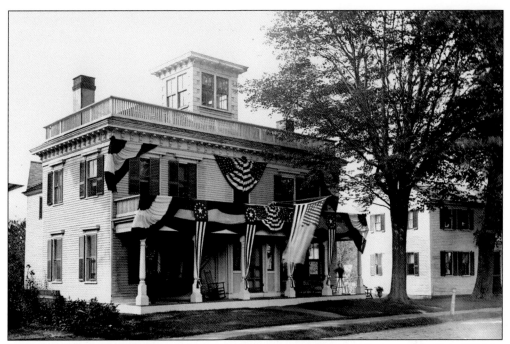

ITALIANATE HOUSE ON PLEASANT STREET. This home at 21 Pleasant Street was built in 1825 by Richard Gilpatric. The residence was later owned by Judge Edward E. Bourne. (64.8.235.)

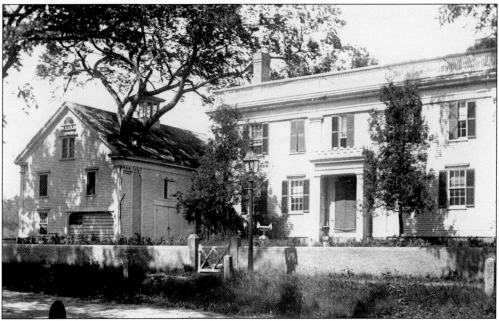

THE STORER MANSION. This grand home was built in 1758 by Joseph A. Storer. Joseph enlisted to fight in the Revolutionary War in 1777, but shortly thereafter he became sick. He died in Albany, N.Y. Storer's son Joseph inherited the property, and he notably welcomed President Monroe to the home in 1817 and General Lafayette in 1825. The first barn on the property was built in 1855 and purposely enclosed a large elm tree. The barn was torn down in 1929. (84L.159.a.)

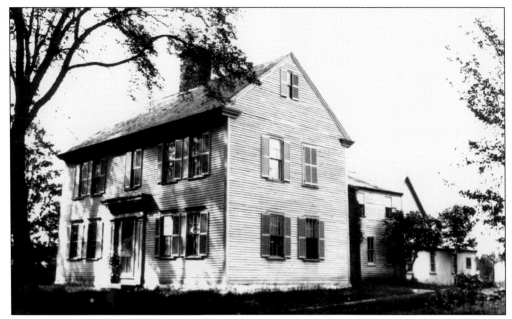

SITE OF SUMMER STREET MURDER. This home at 63 Summer Street was once owned by Dr. Charles Swett. Dr. Swett was murdered by his wife, Jane, who had poisoned a bottle of liquor her husband had hidden in the barn. Jane Swett was sentenced to six years in prison. After serving her sentence, she returned to Kennebunk and lived at the poor farm, where she eventually died. Mrs. Swett was buried next to her husband in Evergreen Cemetery. (84.L.415.)

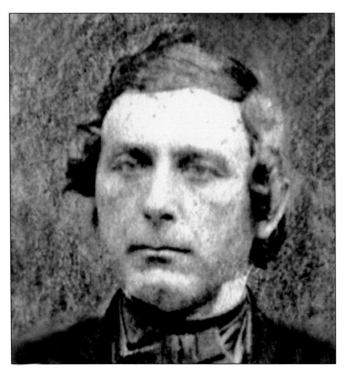

DR. CHARLES SWETT. Dr. Swett practiced as a physician but he had no formal medical training. At his wife's trial it was brought to light that, before his demise, Dr. Swett had a serious drinking problem, fought frequently with his wife, abused drugs, and was reportedly having an affair with another woman. (Trial of Jane Swett book 1363.)

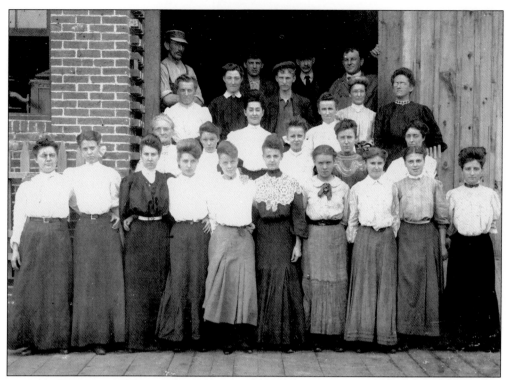

FACTORY WORKERS. These workers—most of them women—were employed *c.* 1905 at the Goodall Matting Company, located on the corner of Main and Storer Streets. (1993.26.)

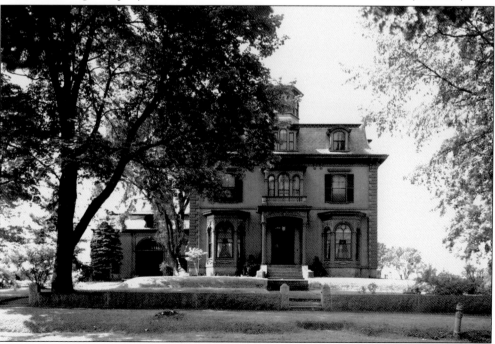

67 SUMMER STREET. Seen here is the George Wise House, which was built in 1868. The house was the first in Kennebunk to have steam heat. (89.34.102.a.)

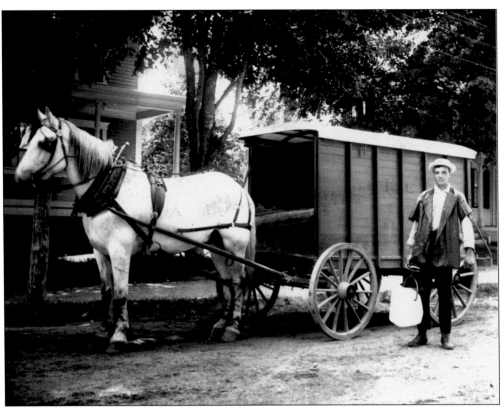

AN ICE DELIVERY MAN ON PLEASANT STREET. On hot summer days, children regularly followed behind the ice carts in hopes of getting a piece of chipped ice. (K272.)

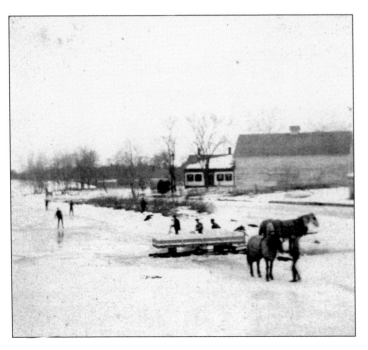

ICE HARVESTING ON THE MOUSAM RIVER. Ice was typically harvested in January and February, and then was packed and stored in sawdust before being sold throughout the summer. One advertisement in 1899 offered "Real Ice: no fancy colors or swampy taste." Ice was also harvested from a pond behind the Parker Wiggin Home on Fletcher Street and from many other ponds across York County. (64.8.250.)

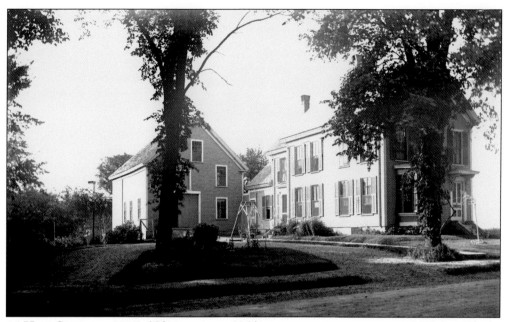

16 High Street c. 1905. (Glass negative 226.)

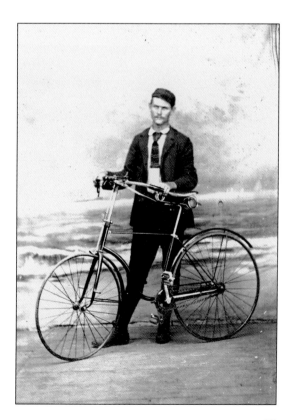

George Mitchell and His Bike. (1998.67.3.6.)

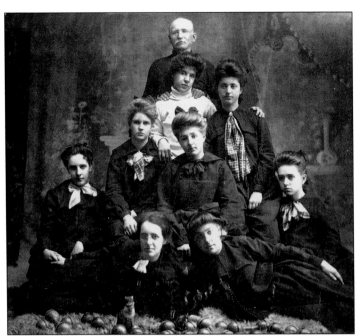

WILLIAM GOODWIN'S ATHLETIC CLUB. Goodwin (back row, center), a builder by trade, also held a number of athletic classes in the upstairs of the Kelly-Warren Block. He instructed both young women and men. Standing directly in front of Mr. Williams is Mabel Kelley, one of his students, who became a well-known historian of her day. William Goodwin was also a Civil War veteran, serving in the 11th Regiment, Maine Infantry.

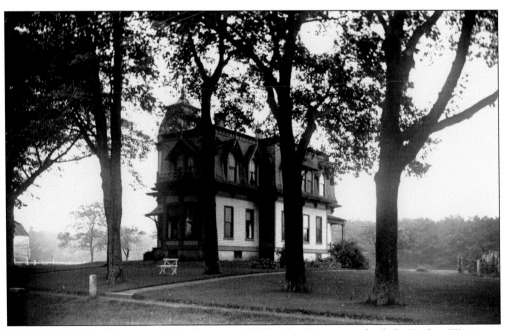

FLETCHER STREET VICTORIAN. This home at 59 Fletcher Street was built by Parker Wiggin at the turn of the 20th century. Behind the residence there was a large barn, and in the winter, an ice pond where blocks of ice were harvested. (K1059.)

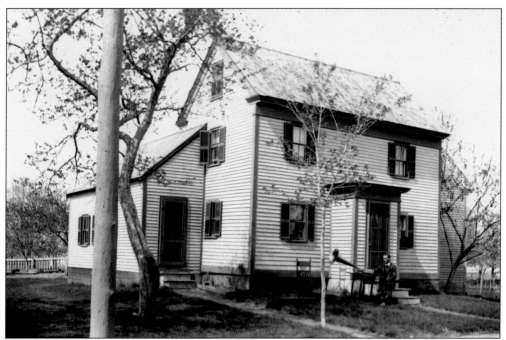

MUSIC ON FLETCHER STREET. This image from a glass-plate negative by Albion Moody shows the home at 50 Fletcher Street, which was across the street from the Moody house. On this day a man sits beside his Victrola on the front lawn. This home was built prior to 1860 and its original owner is unknown. At one time the residence was owned by a Civil War soldier, Harrison Sargent, who was the adopted son of N. K. Sargent. (85.L.430.)

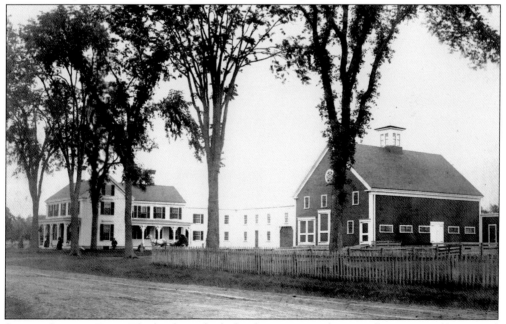

SAMUEL STEVENS FARM. The land on which this farm now stands originally was owned by Samuel Stevens, who built a small Cape-style house on the property in 1797. That home was torn down and the present structure was built in 1854 by Ithamar Littlefield. (Glass negative 228.)

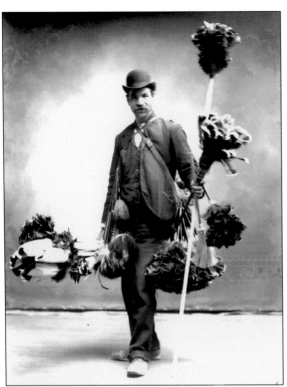

A Chimney Sweep. This unidentified chimney sweep was photographed by Albion Moody c. 1900. (78M.j.410.)

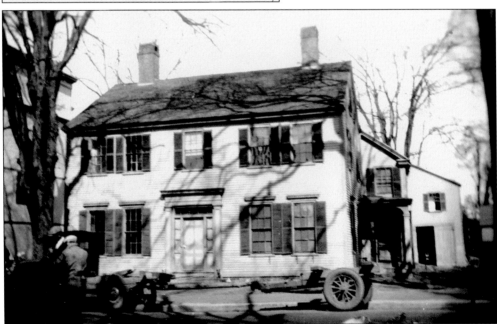

The Stephen Furbish House. Built in 1797 at the corner of Main Street and Bourne Street, this house was sold to Capt. John Hill in 1858. He lived in the east side of the residence, and Andrew Walker lived in the Bourne Street side. In 1904 Hill's widow left the house to the Baptist Church to be used as a parsonage. It was razed in 1930 to make way for a Texaco station. The Texaco station was demolished in 1984 and an X'tra Mart was built in its place. (85.12.5.11.a.)

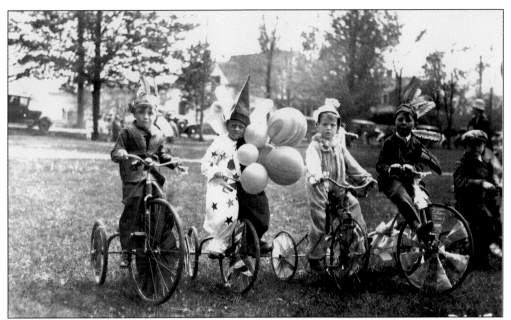

HEALTH PARADE RIDERS. Young tricycle riders line up during the 1928 Health Parade. (73.36.b.)

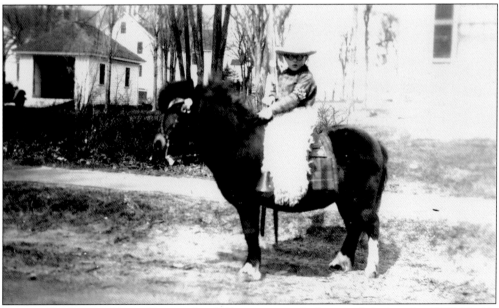

YOUNG HORSEMAN, BILLY BINDER JR. Billy poses astride his steed during the 1928 Health Parade. Billy's father, William, of West Kennebunk, was also a horseman. The elder Binder traveled with the "Wild West Show" as a fancy rider and roper. (K242.)

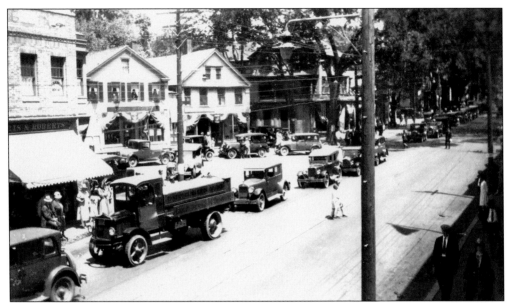

MAIN STREET KENNEBUNK. This a postcard view that dates from about 1930. Note the long line of traffic. We often think this kind of summer traffic is a *modern* headache, but tourism was in full swing even in this era. (Private Collection.)

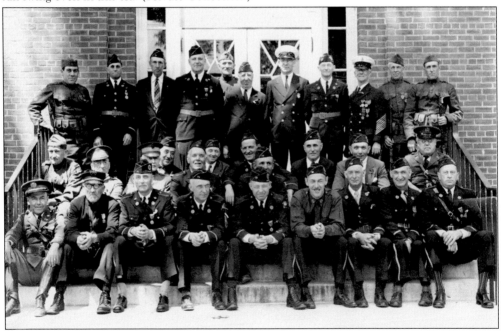

VETERANS' PORTRAIT. This photograph was taken on Memorial Day 1938. From left to right are the following: (first row) Woodbury Stevens, George Wallace, Ralph Evans, Joe Burke, Hollis Pruscott, "Hoddie" Day, Franke Burke, Edmund Burke, and Earl Smith; (second row—in order given, one name is missing) Leslie Boston, Roy Evans, Henry Parsons, J. Carver, Turk Rand, John Gooch, Bert Galucia, George Cooper, Joe Polito, and George Eaton; (third row) Ernest Hatch, Roy Junkins, John Hawkins, Reg Harford, Charles McDonald, Roy Clark, Carl Edwards, Floyd Junkins, Joe Francisco, Charles Smith, and "Jeff" Clark. (K616.)

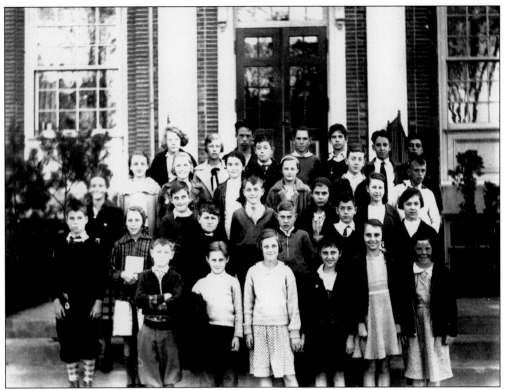

STUDENT BODY. An unidentified group of students poses on the Kennebunk High School steps *c*. 1930. (89.34.58.)

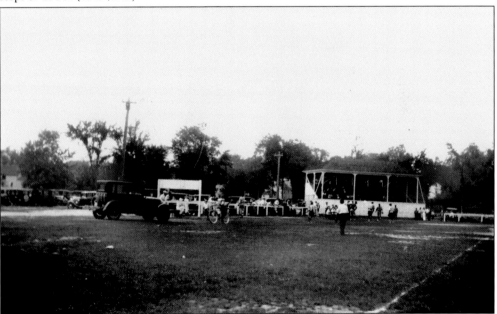

THE OLD GRANDSTAND. This vintage image shows the grandstand located on Parsons Field, at Park and Dane Streets, as it appeared *c*. 1930. The grandstand was a gift of Mr. Henry Parsons. (K175.)

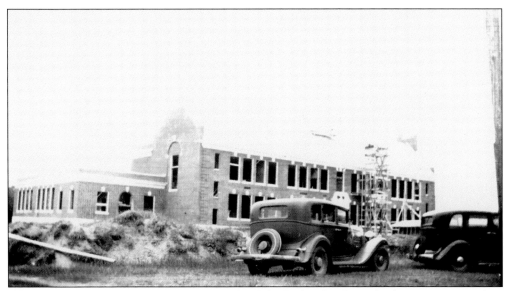

KENNEBUNK HIGH SCHOOL. This photograph of the high school on Fletcher Street was taken while the building was under construction in 1939. (Mabel Kelley collection BSM.)

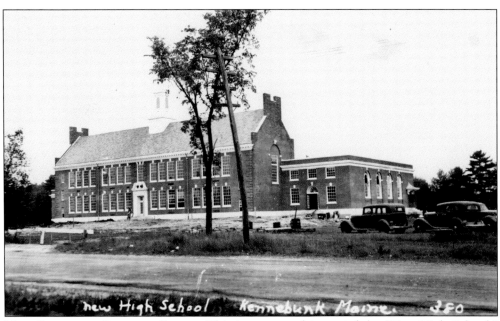

NEW SCHOOL ON FLETCHER STREET. This is a postcard image of the "New High School." The building was constructed in 1939 and still serves the community as the high school. (Private collection.)

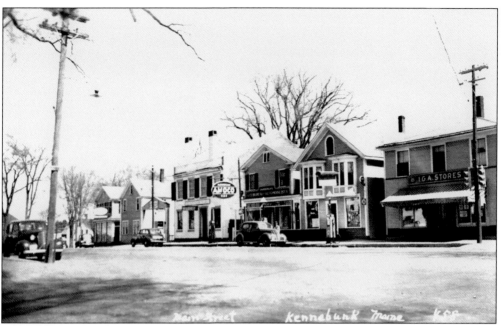

BRICK STORE MUSEUM BLOCK C. 1930. (Private Collection.)

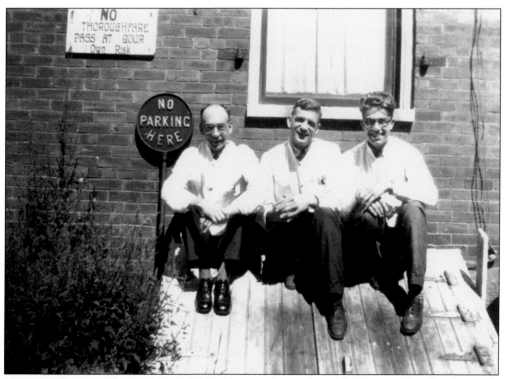

TAKING A BREAK. Gilman Fiske (left), Bill Gowen (center), and P. Gowen take a break outside the Fiske drugstore, which was located in the Ross Block on Main Street. (1991-12.10.7.)

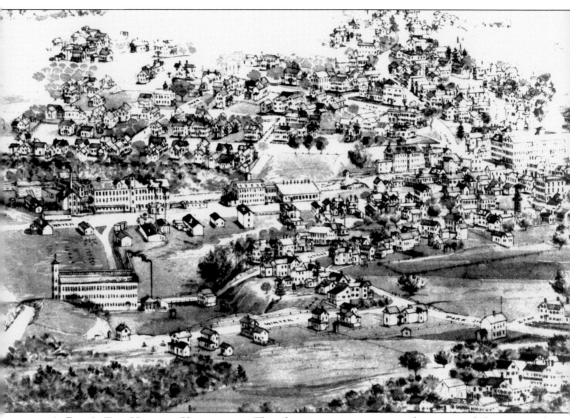

A BIRD'S-EYE VIEW OF KENNEBUNK. This drawing is an accurate depiction of the town of Kennebunk as it was in 1895. The Shoe Counter Factory below Winter Street can be seen, as can the Leatheroid factories that spanned the Mousam River. The Swan Street School and the Mousam House still existed at that date and are included in the drawing as well. (1992.i.56.3.a.)

Four

THE LANDING

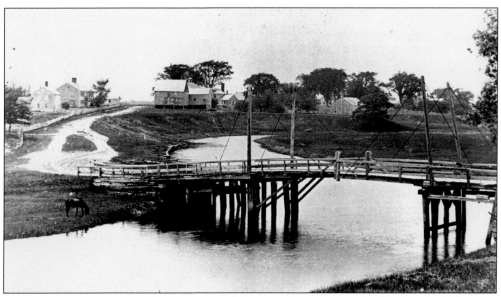

DURRELL'S BRIDGE. This bridge was named for an early settler of this locale, which lost two families to Indian attacks. The first mention of the name Durrell's Bridge appears in town records of 1765. (84.L.195.b.)

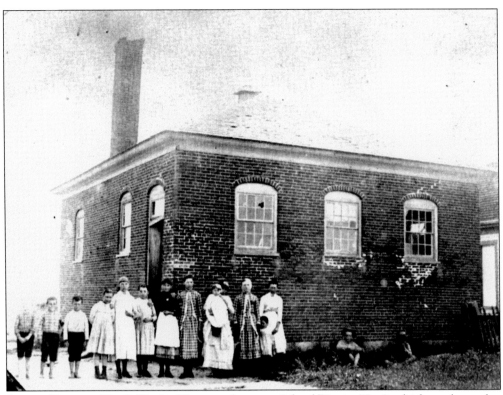

SCHOOL DISTRICT NO. 2. The building seen here was School District No. 2, which was located at 143 Summer Street. This old school was built in 1820, was remodeled in 1850, and remained in use until it was razed in 1887. A new wooden school was erected at the same site. (85.12.5.52.)

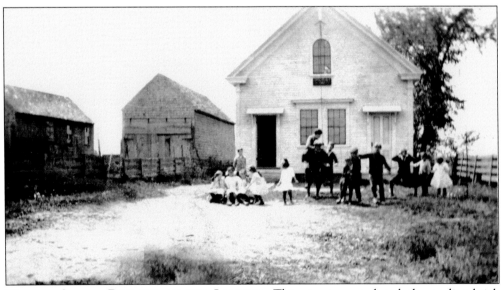

WOODEN SCHOOL BUILDING AT THE LANDING. This structure replaced the earlier brick schoolhouse at the Landing. The wooden school building was closed in 1939, and later was converted into a private residence. (1993.47.3.a.)

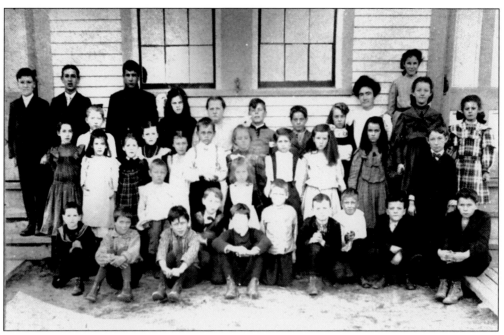

STUDENTS AT THE LANDING SCHOOLHOUSE. An unidentified group of students sit for a class picture outside the school at the Landing *c.* 1915. (1993.I.38.)

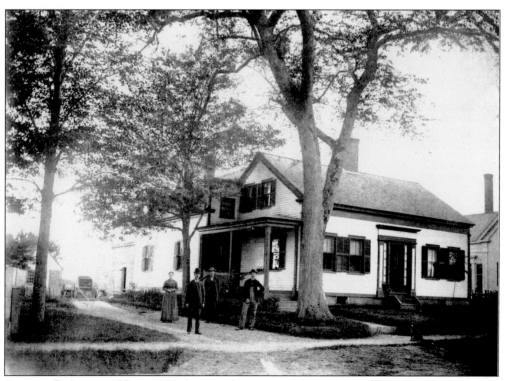

ARTELLE R. JELLISON HOME, 154 SUMMER STREET. Members of the Jellison family are pictured outside their residence. (Private Collection.)

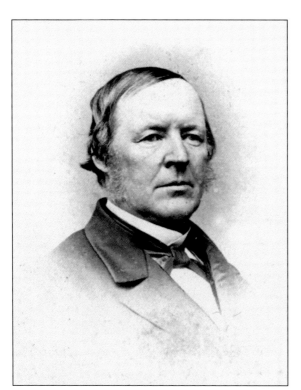

HUGH McCULLOCH. The secretary of the treasury under Pres. Abraham Lincoln was Hugh McCulloch, a native of Kennebunk, Maine. (People File BSM.)

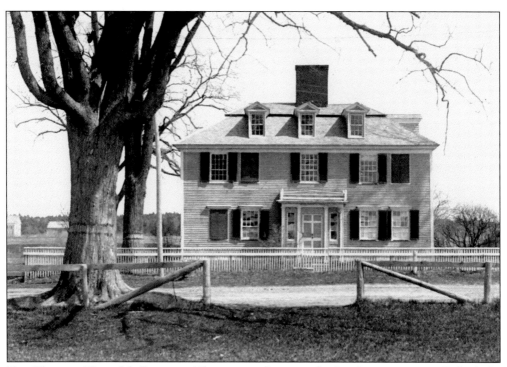

THE HOME OF HUGH McCULLOCH. This ancient house at the Landing was originally built for Dr. Thatcher Goddard in 1782, and was sold to McCulloch in 1801. (84.L.164.2.)

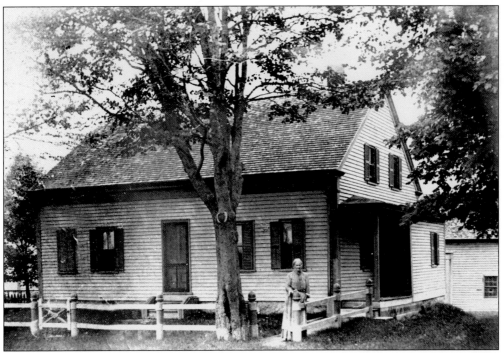

98 Summer Street. The G. B. Littlefield House on Summer Street was built *c.* 1856. (85.L.38.)

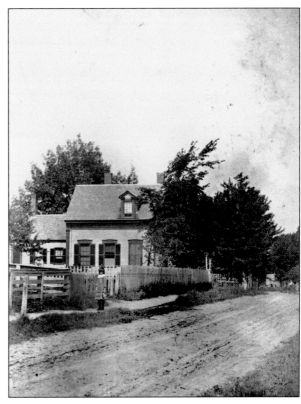

129 Summer Street. Seen here is the home of Emily Francis Durrell Day. (90.44.36.b.)

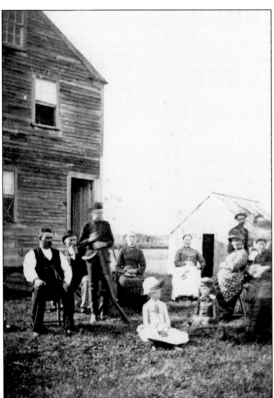

Durrell Family Reunion. This photograph was taken during the family reunion held at the Durrell Homestead c. 1880. Among those present are Francis Emery, Charles Durrell, Nancy Durrell, Sarah Fuller, Edith Emery, and Florence Burbank. (90.44.8.)

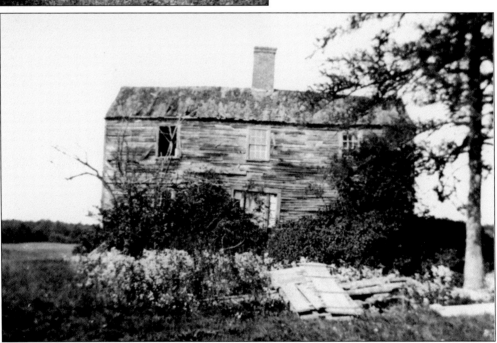

The Durrell Homestead at the Landing. Luckily, Edith Furbish captured this image of the old and vacant Durrell Homestead prior to its collapse. The homestead was located on the Arundel side of the Kennebunk River. (90.44.9.)

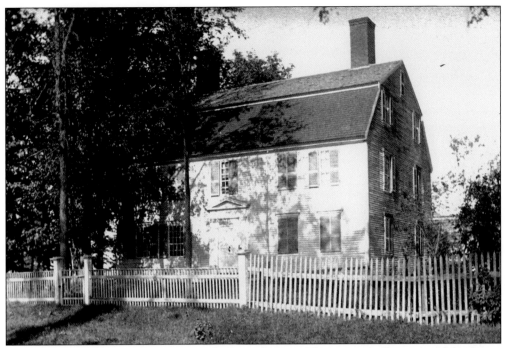

The Theodore Lyman Home at 110 Summer Street. The original ell portion of this home was built in the 1750s, and the three-story addition was constructed in 1784. (BSM Photo Album 2871.)

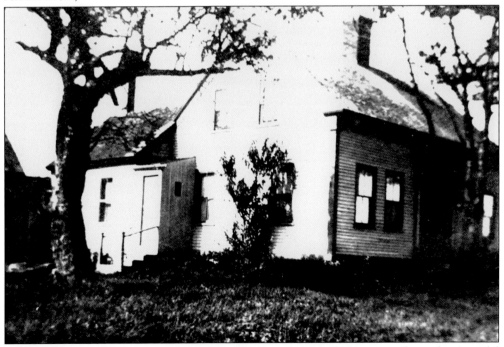

Joseph Durrell Home at the Landing. The Joseph Durrell Home stands on the Arundel side of the Kennebunk River and is now known as the Red House. Durrell was a ship's carpenter. (90.44.5.)

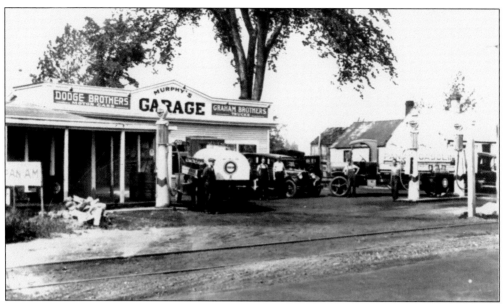

KENNEBUNK LANDING GARAGE. The garage building (at left) was erected in 1926. This c. 1935 photograph shows Graham Brothers Trucks, Dodge Brothers Motor Cars, and Murphy's Garage. A. H. Murphy was the proprietor at the time. (1993.i.38.14.2.)

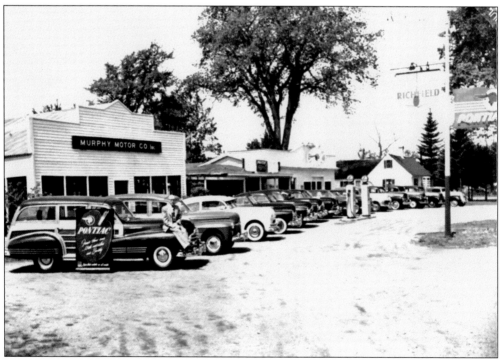

LATER VIEW OF LANDING GARAGE. Murphy's Motor Company occupied the garage c. 1945, when this photograph was taken. The garage is currently home to Jim's Service Center. (1993.i.38.14.3.)

Five

LOWER VILLAGE

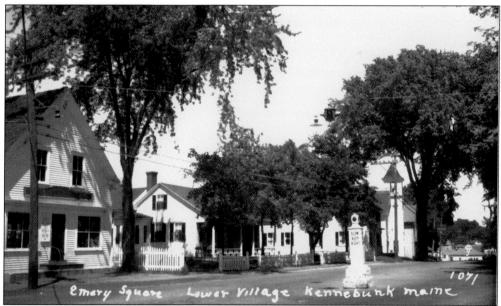

Emery Square   Lower Village   Kennebunk, Maine
1071

THE OLD SQUARE, LOWER VILLAGE. This is a view of Emery Square, in Lower Village, Kennebunk. The square was named for Isaac Emery, a Civil War veteran who operated a store in this vicinity. In 1872 there were 13 Emery families living in Lower Village. This *c.* 1930 image shows the Washington Hose Company. On the left is the building that now houses Poof Berries toy store. At some point this building was moved back on the lot. (Author's Collection.)

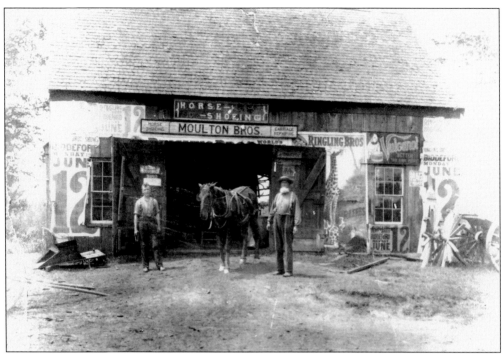

THE MOULTON BROTHERS' BLACKSMITH SHOP. In this 1908 photograph, Jackson Moulton (left) and Ansel Boothby stand outside the blacksmith shop in Lower Village. (89.34.136.)

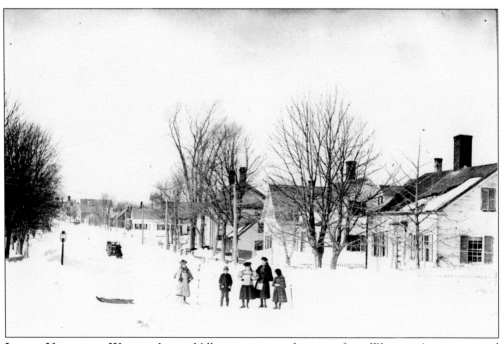

LOWER VILLAGE IN WINTER. Lower Village is seen in this view from Western Avenue toward Kennebunk. In the distance is the steeple of the Advent church. (BSM Photo Album 80.L.88.)

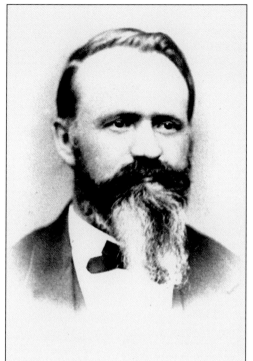 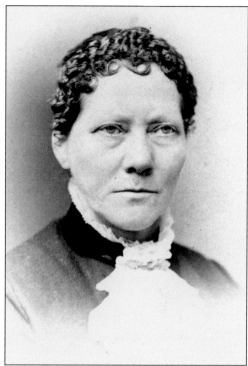

LEFT: SETH BRYANT, 1826–1888. Bryant was born in Rochester, Massachusetts, and later wed Mary E. Wormwood of Kennebunk. (BSM Photo Album 80.L.88.) **RIGHT: MARY E. WORMWOOD BRYANT.** (BSM Photo Album 80.L.88.)

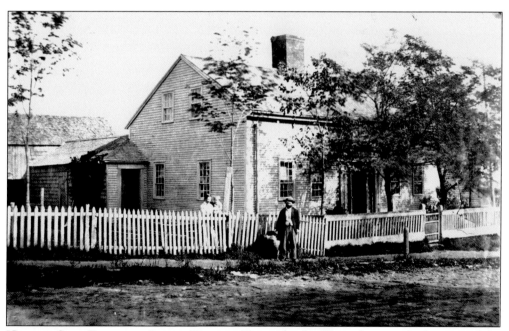

HOME OF SETH BRYANT IN LOWER VILLAGE. Currently, the Bryant home is the location of the Ron Goyette Studio. (BSM Photo Album 80.L.88.)

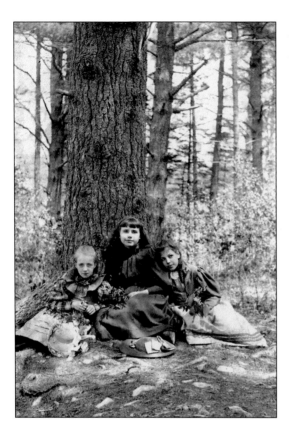

A NATURE POSE. Pictured here are young Addie Bryant, Mary Ward, and Addie Willard of Lower Village, Kennebunk. (BSM Photo Album 80.L.88.)

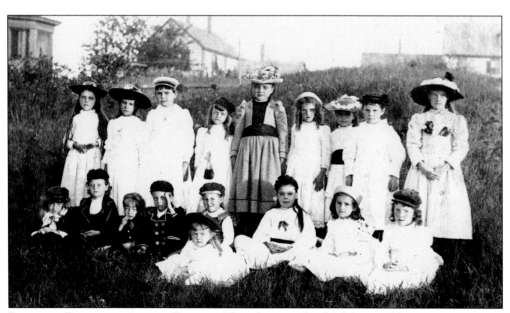

BIRTHDAY PARTY FOR ADELINE BRYANT. This photograph of Adeline and her party guests was taken in Lower Village, Kennebunk, in 1892. (BSM Photo Album 80.L.88.)

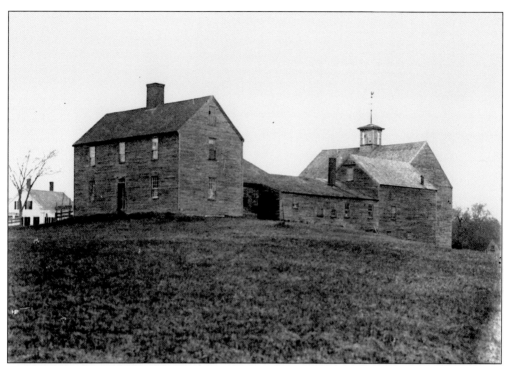

Lower Village, the Mitchell Garrison. These are two images of the John Mitchell Garrison, which stood on the site of the present-day Franciscan Monastery in Lower Village, Kennebunk. The garrison house was erected about 1745. The first vessel built on the Kennebunk River was raised at John Mitchell's wharf in 1755 by John Bourne. (84.L.205.2 & 84.L.205.1.)

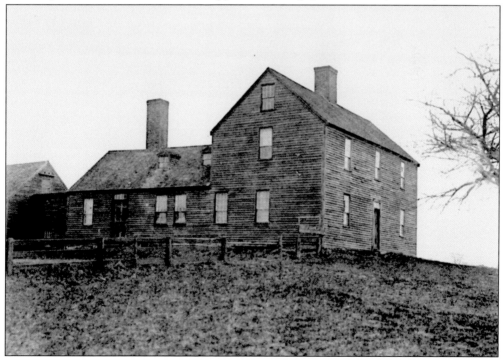

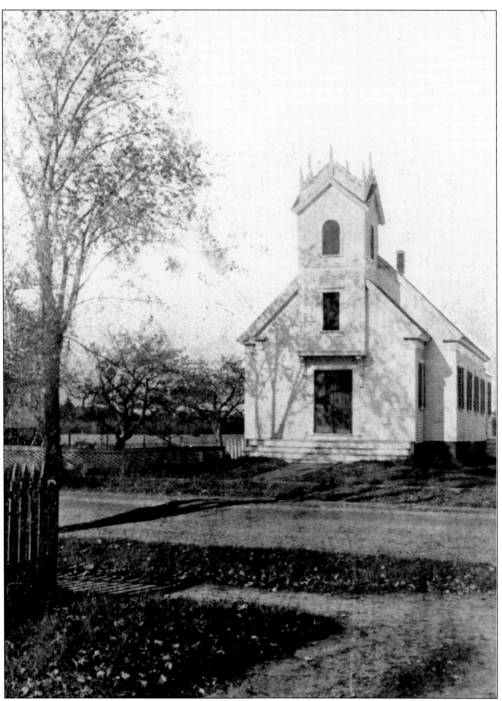

ADVENT CHRISTIAN CHURCH IN LOWER VILLAGE. This church was built in 1852. Leading members of its congregation were Capt. Elisha Mitchell, Clement Littlefield, Benjamin Emery, William Mitchell, Jonas Merrill, and Benjamin Merrill. The church's dedication was held on June 27, 1852, with the Rev. Edwin P. Burnham presiding. (Author's Collection.)

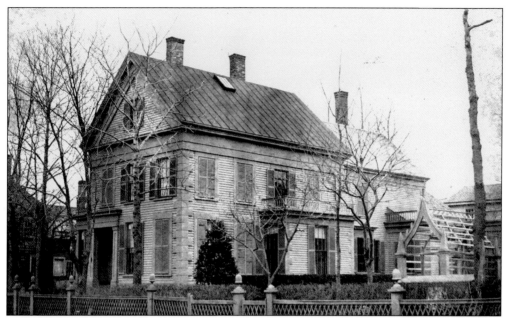

LOWER VILLAGE HOME. This photograph, donated to the Brick Store Museum by a former owner of the home pictured, shows the residence as it once appeared at the corner of Route 9 and Beach Avenue. In its prime, the house was surrounded by extensive gardens. The property is now the site of the Kings Port Inn at Lower Village. (2003.059.0004.)

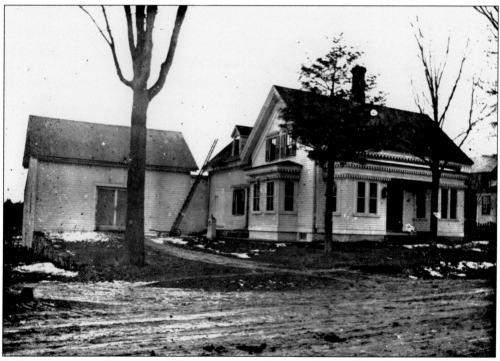

9 BEACH AVENUE. This Lower Village home was photographed *c.* 1900. (Private Collection.)

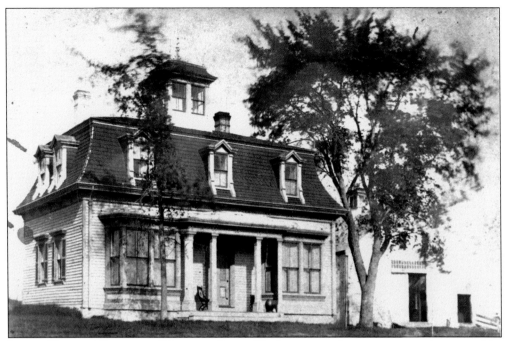

LOWER VILLAGE HOME WITH MANSARD ROOF. The home seen here was at one time owned by Sarah F. Emery and later by Richard Talpey. (1992.i.129.2.)

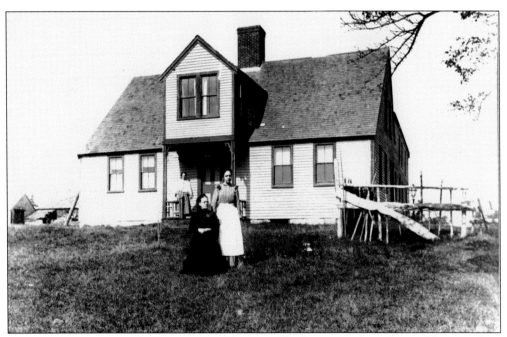

THE JOTHAM MITCHELL HOME AT LOWER VILLAGE. This home stands on Route 35, across from Old Port Road. Known as the Mitchell Homestead, it was an icon of Lower Village in the early 1900s. Images of the homestead also appeared on tourist postcards. (1993.i.177.10.a.)

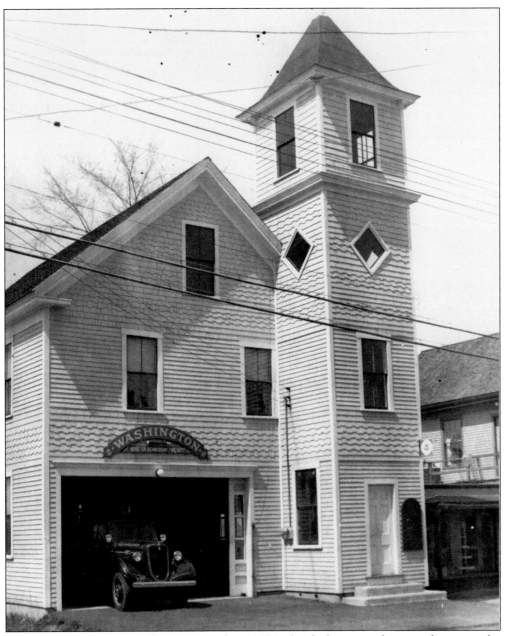

WASHINGTON HOSE FIRE COMPANY. Built *c.* 1876, the firehouse used to stand next to the present-day H. B. Provisions store. The structure was demolished in March 1972 to make room for a parking lot. (K538.)

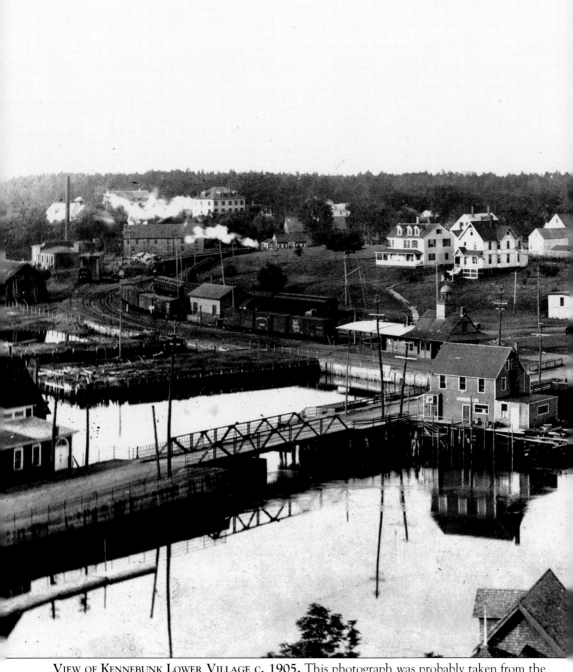

VIEW OF KENNEBUNK LOWER VILLAGE C. **1905.** This photograph was probably taken from the

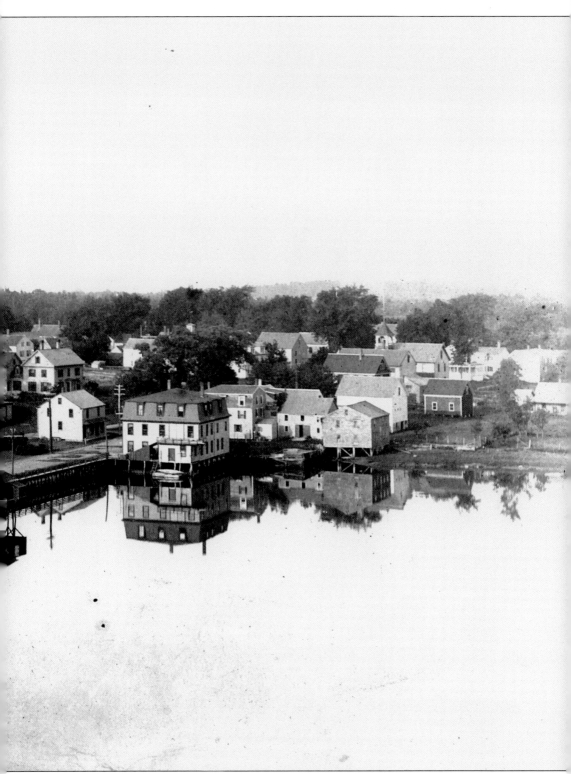

steeple of the South Congregational church in Kennebunkport. (K255.)

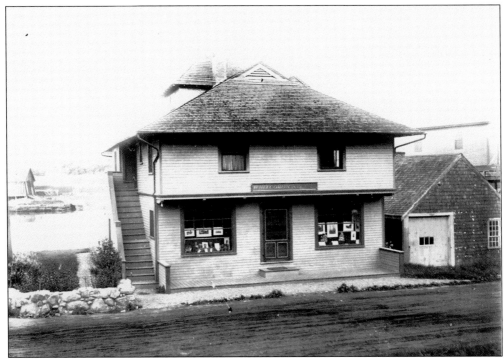

THE PHOTOGRAPHIC STUDIO OF B. J. WHITCOMB. Whitcomb's studio is shown here, on the bridge spanning the Kennebunk River at Lower Village. (84.L.255.1.)

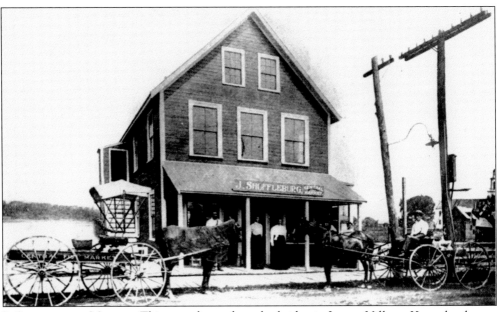

J. SHUFFLEBURG MARKET. This store located on the bridge in Lower Village, Kennebunk, was built by Captain Heckman. (64.7.220.)

Six

WEST KENNEBUNK

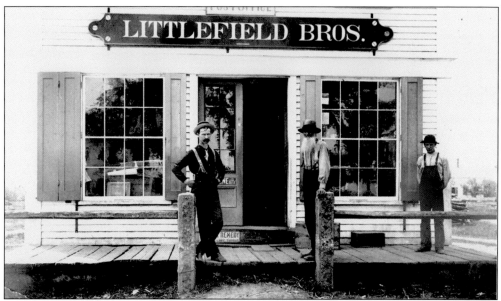

THE LITTLEFIELD BROTHERS' STORE. This image of the West Kennebunk store dates from about 1890. This building was also the home of the post office. Standing on the left is one of the Littlefield brothers, and on the right is a man named Joe Tripp, who was known as a handyman about town. The second floor of this building was used as a Good Templars hall. (K1104.)

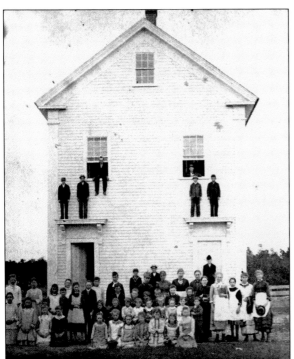

WEST KENNEBUNK SCHOOL. This schoolhouse in West Kennebunk was built in 1850 and was destroyed by fire on September 26, 1881. It was determined that the fire had been deliberately set as both ends of the structure had been saturated with kerosene. This school was known as District No. 9. (K727A.)

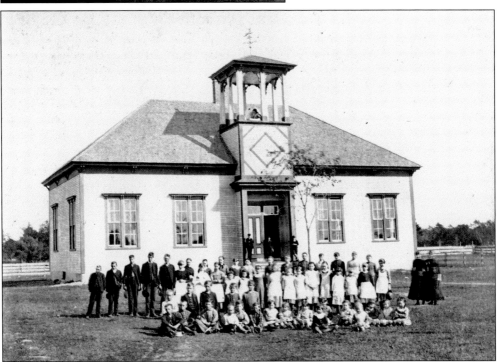

NEW DISTRICT NO. 9 SCHOOL. Following the destruction of the school in the previous photograph, a new school was built a short time later. Years after it had ceased to be used as a school, this building was sold to the York Lodge for $1,500, and it is still used as a Masonic hall today. (Private Collection.)

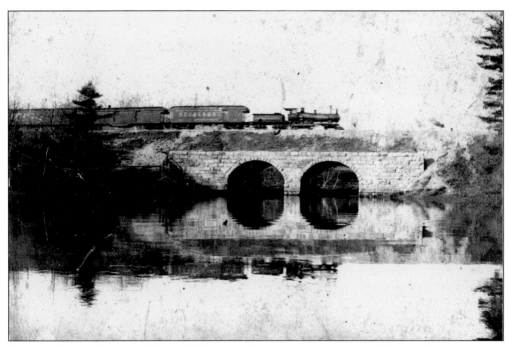

MOUSAM RIVER TRESTLE. This *c.* 1880 image shows a train crossing the Mousam River trestle in West Kennebunk. The photograph was taken from the Twine Mill. (1979.)

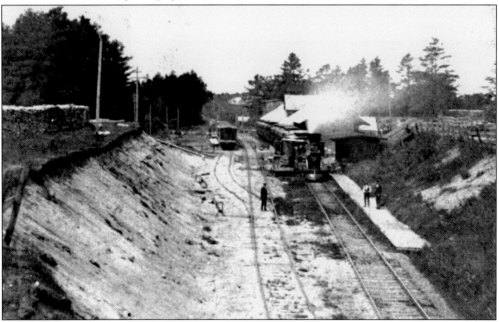

WEST KENNEBUNK RAILROAD DEPOT. The first passage of a train through this station was in 1842. Samuel Mitchell was the depot's first station agent, and he was succeeded by Ivory Littlefield, who held the position for many years. This station was a busy place until the railroad expanded to Kennebunk in 1873. Many farmers in West Kennebunk sold wood to be used in the wood-burning locomotives of the era. All traffic on this line was discontinued sometime between 1942 and 1944, and the rails were removed. (84.L.522.)

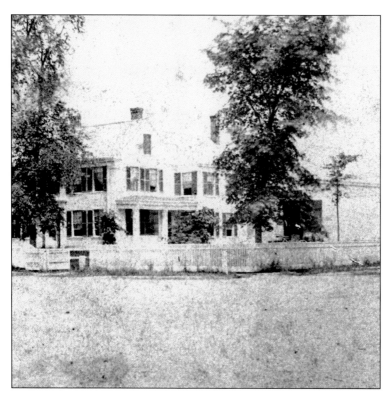

WEST KENNEBUNK HOME. This is a stereoview of the George Perkins Homestead, which was located at the corner of Warrens Way and Main Street. Warrens Way was once known as Pleasant Street and was also called "Sneak Street" for many years. (84.L.513.)

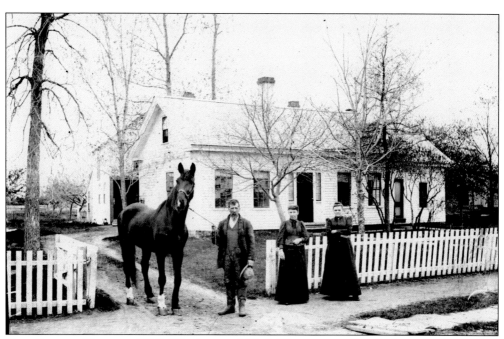

OTIS PERKINS HOME C. 1880. The home of Civil War veteran Otis Perkins was located on Main Street in West Kennebunk. Standing in front of the residence are, from left to right, Perkins's horse "Duke"; Otis; his wife, Elmira; and Cora Gowen. (85.L.60.)

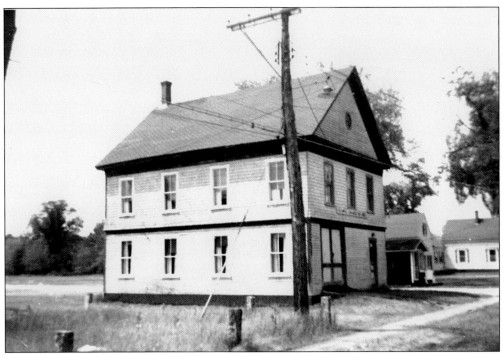

THE ALEWIVE GRANGE HALL OF WEST KENNEBUNK. The hall was built in the fall of 1886, at a cost of $1,000. The structure is now a residence. (84.L.322.)

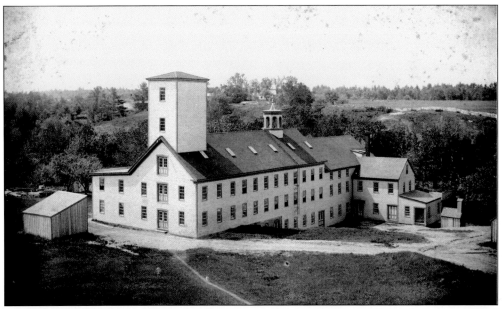

THE MITCHELL GRISTMILL. The gristmill was constructed in the late 1700s, and was later owned by Robert Lord, who turned it into a twine mill. This mill was illuminated by whale oil lamps when it was first built. In 1922 the wooden mill was torn down and a brick mill was erected in its place. (K564.)

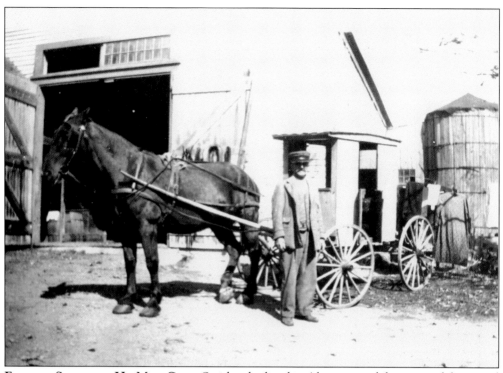

ELBRIDGE SMITH AND HIS MAIL CART. Smith, who lived in Alewive, used this cart to deliver mail on the West Kennebunk RFD (Rural Free Delivery) route between 1902 and 1932. (4116.)

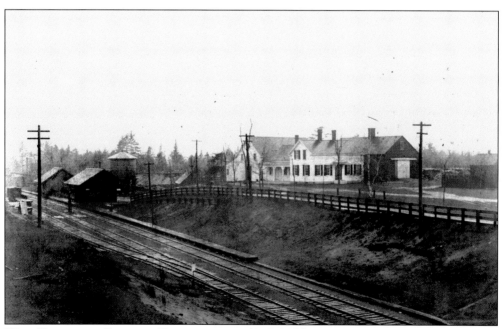

WEST KENNEBUNK RAILROAD DEPOT C. 1870. (84.L.295.)

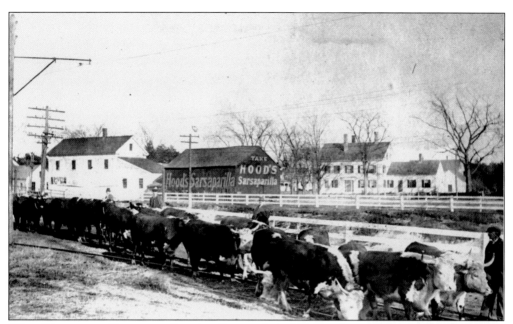

WEST KENNEBUNK ROUNDUP. Seen herding cattle in 1914 are Ernest Mason, George Authier, Tom Goodwin, and Edward Littlefield. In the background of this West Kennebunk scene is the Mitchell Home on Mill Street. On the left is the store owned by the Littlefield brothers. (Private Collection.)

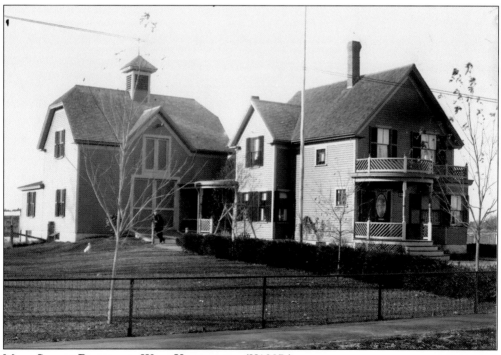

MAIN STREET RESIDENCE, WEST KENNEBUNK. (K1007.)

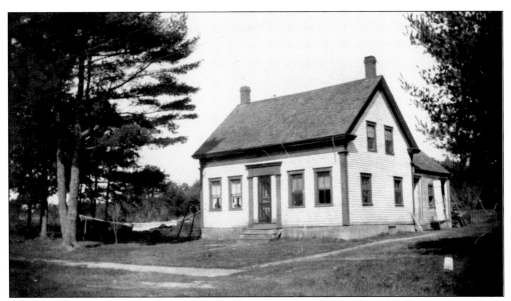

WILLIAM HATCH HOME. This home at 75 Fletcher Street, West Kennebunk, now has a large front porch. (2004.046.0001.)

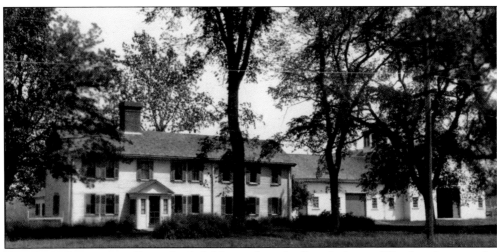

THE JACOB LITTLEFIELD FARM. Littlefield served in the Revolutionary War for nine months, and built this West Kennebunk house c. 1780. He and his wife, Abigail, left the home to their daughter Sarah, who married Oliver Perkins Sr. Perkins opened a tavern for the accommodation of travelers and also operated a bar at the south end of the structure. In 1854 Oliver lost both arms and one eye in an accident that happened while he was firing a cannon at a memorial service. He regained his health and led a successful business until he died in 1856. The farm remained in the same family until 1940. (84.L.289.)

Seven

ALEWIVE

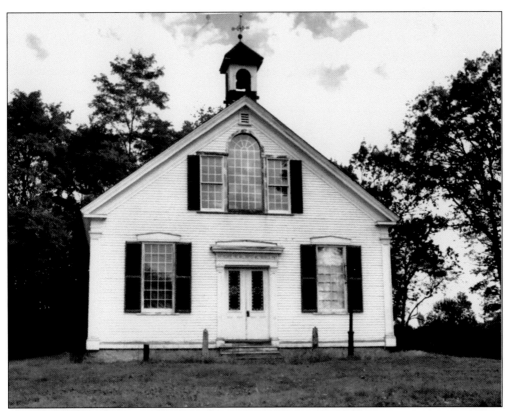

THE FREE WILL BAPTIST CHURCH. This church was constructed on or near the site of the Alewive meetinghouse of 1796. The original meetinghouse had been built by Alewive residents because it was difficult for them to make the journey to the First Parish meetinghouse in Kennebunk. In 1803 many local residents organized a church among themselves, and Joshua Roberts Jr. was ordained as their minister. This church was built for the congregation in 1847. (Author's Collection.)

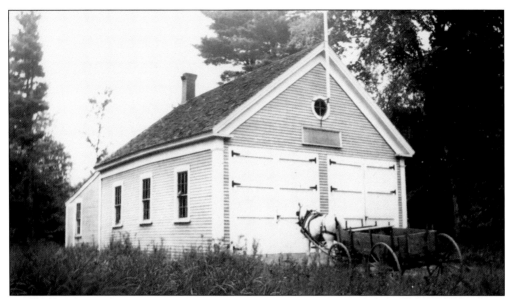

ONE-ROOM SCHOOL. Built in 1855, District No. 7 is across the road from the Smith Farm in Alewive. Eventually school operations there were discontinued, and the building became a bus barn in 1941. The structure is still standing and is now privately owned. (Mabel Kelley Collection.)

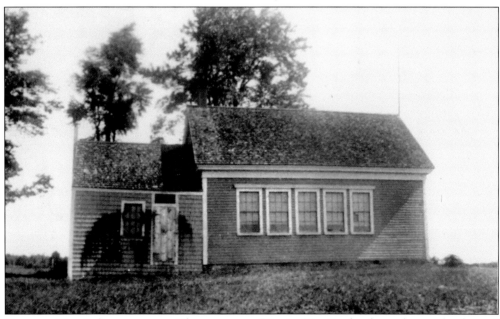

DISTRICT NO. 8 SCHOOLHOUSE. The one-room District No. 8 school stood near the farm of Sargent Day, which was called Willow Lane. Both buildings were destroyed in the fire of 1947. (Private Collection.)

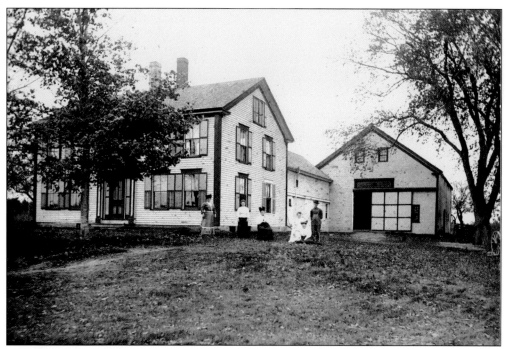

THE WARD BROTHERS' HOME. This Alewive residence, built *c.* 1825, was home to various people over the years, including John Burnham, Ezra Smith, Ivory Smith, Theodore Webber, and the Hill family. (84.L.222.)

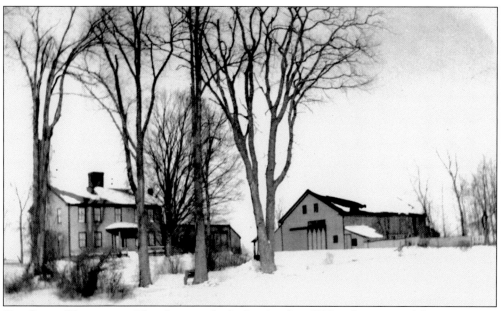

THE SMITH HOMESTEAD. This farm was built shortly after 1753 and was owned for generations by the Smith family. (Mabel Kelley Collection.)

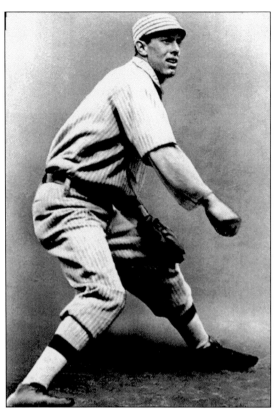

JOHN WESLEY COOMBS, 1882–1957.
John Wesley Coombs was better known as the legendary baseball pitcher "Colby Jack Coombs." After graduating from Colby College in 1906, he was signed as a Major League pitcher with Connie Mack's Philadelphia Athletics. Coombs beat the Chicago Cubs three times in the 1910 World Series. He moved on to pitch for Brooklyn from 1915 to 1918, managed the Philadelphia Phillies in 1919, and served as pitching coach for the Detroit Tigers in 1920. Coombs later coached at Williams College, Princeton University, and Duke University. In 1909 he and his family moved to the Alewive farm shown below. During vacations Coombs enjoyed spending time at the family farm. (Nelson Wentworth.)

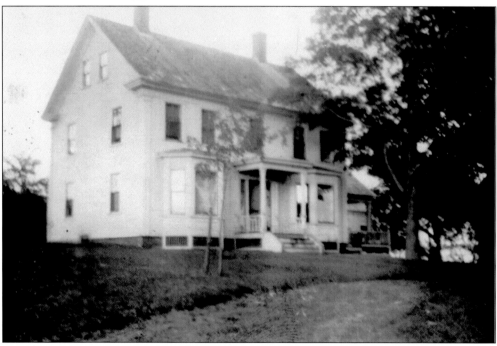

THE COOMBS FARM IN ALEWIVE. This house was originally built by the Burnham family after the land was deeded to them in 1754. (Nelson Wentworth.)

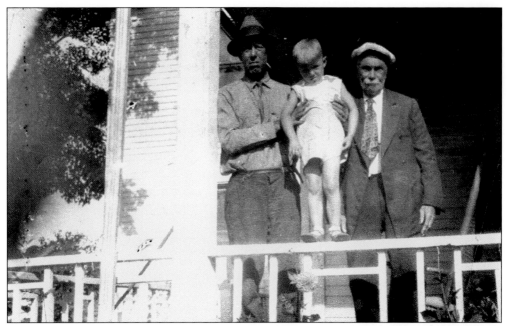

Time with Family. Jack Coombs (left) visits with his father, Frank Coombs (right), on the porch of their Alewive home. The youngster is Jack's grandnephew Donald Wentworth. (Nelson Wentworth.)

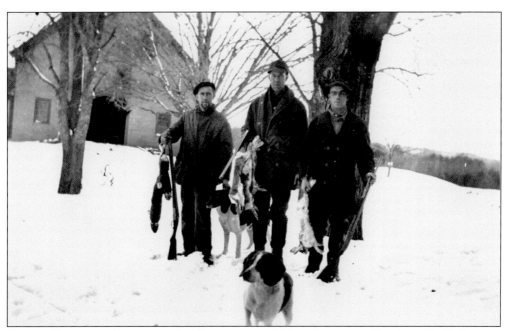

Coombs Brothers. Seen returning from a successful hunting trip are brothers Curtis Coombs (left), Jack Coombs (center), and Harry Coombs. (Nelson Wentworth.)

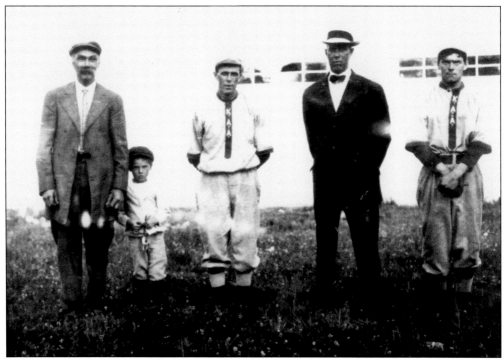

THREE GENERATIONS OF BASEBALL ENTHUSIASTS. From left to right are Frank Coombs, his grandson Bobby Coombs, and three of Frank's sons—Curtis Coombs, Jack Coombs, and Ernest Coombs. (Nelson Wentworth.)

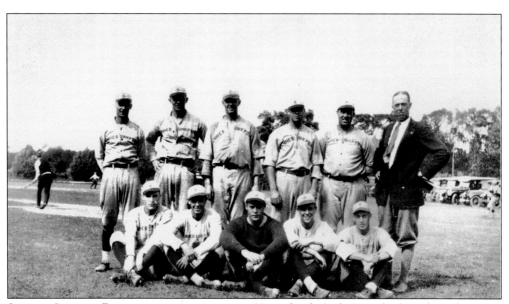

SUMMER LEAGUE. During summer vacations in Kennebunk, Jack Coombs (standing, far right) coached a local baseball team called the Kennebunkport Collegians. This team was made up of vacationing students from many Ivy League colleges and prep schools. (Nelson Wentworth.)

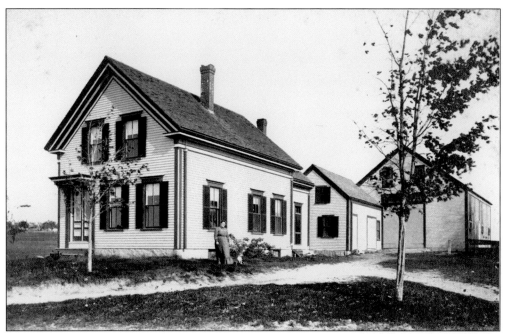

THE ELBRIDGE SMITH HOME. Elbridge Smith built this house *c.* 1877. Shown in the photograph is Ada (Wormwood) Smith, wife of Elbridge. The home is now owned by Ada and Elbridge's granddaughter Anna LeBlanc, and her husband, Arthur. (Anna LeBlanc.)

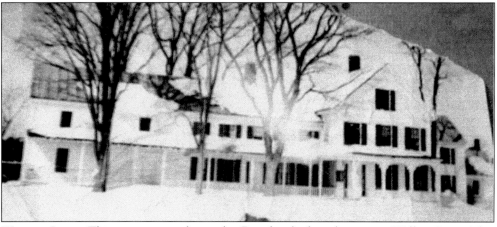

WILLOW LANE. This torn image shows the Day family farm known as Willow Lane. This farm, originally built by Capt. Stephen Day for his son Sargent, burned in the fire of 1947. (Nancy Hooper.)

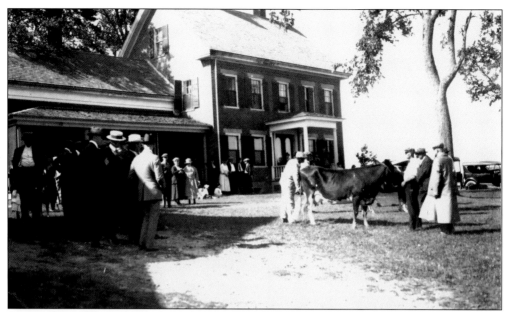

CATTLE SALE. These images from the 1930s show a cattle sale being held at the Pollard Farm. The farm no longer exists. (89.34.160.)

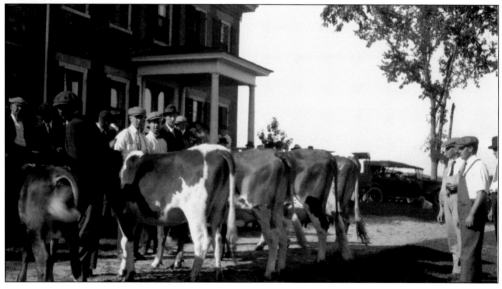

Eight

CAT MOUSAM

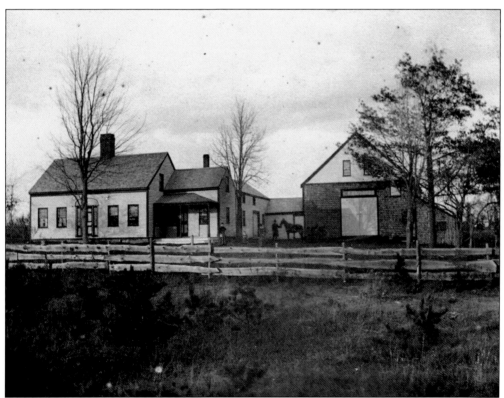

THE GILPATRIC FARM ON CAT MOUSAM ROAD. This farm was purchased by Ivory Gilpatric from Lucretia Dorrance in 1839. At that time there was only a barn standing on the property. Gilpatric subsequently purchased the home of Charles Towne on Lower Brown Street and had that house moved to this site. An ell was then built and a new barn was added in 1854. This photograph was taken *c.* 1880. The ell and barn are no longer standing.

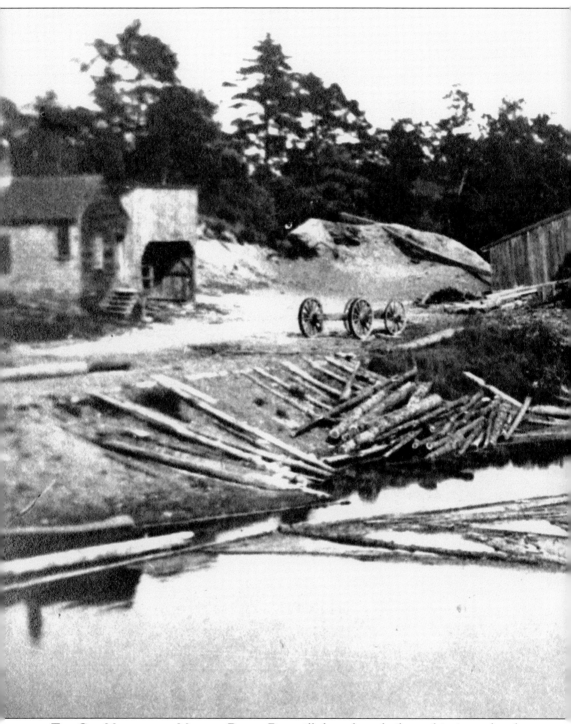

THE CAT MILL ON THE MOUSAM RIVER. Five mills have been built on this site and each was called the Cat Mill. The mills got their name from a storied cat that was owned at the original mill of 1733. There are various legends surrounding the cat, none of which can be proven. One claims the cat had a habit of riding the sled to the saw, and one day got too close to the blade

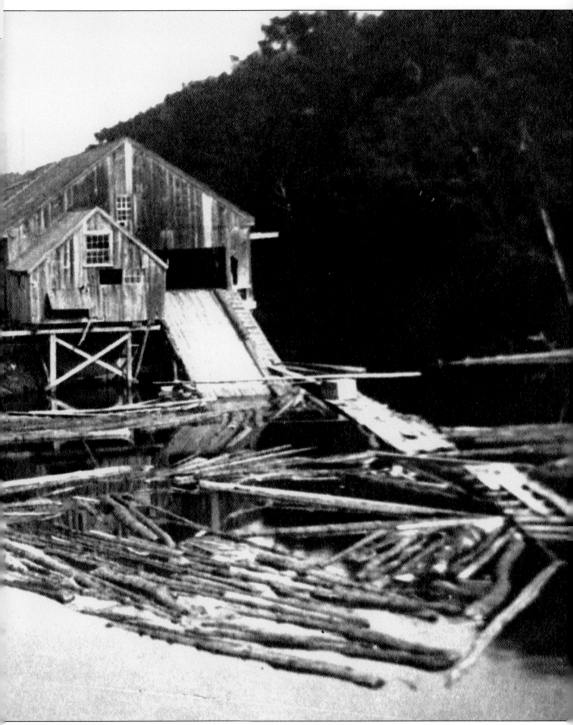

and was killed. Another claims the beloved cat was hung by mischievous kids who played near the mill. Yet another claims the cat was actually a witch. Regardless of the true story, the name Cat Mill has remained. The Cat Mousam Road derives its name from a combination of the terms Cat Mill and Mousam River. (3683 Oversize.)

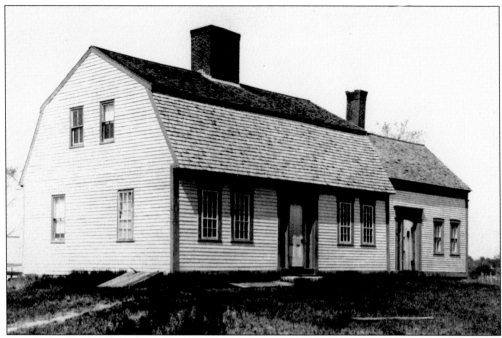

THE KENNEBUNK POOR FARM. The Poor Farm was located on Cat Mousam Road. In 1825 the town purchased the home and land of Abner Cousens and a small piece of abutting property from his father, Nathaniel, to be used for a burying ground. The Poor Farm took in "unfortunates" until about 1897. After that it was used as a "tramp house." According to old town reports, as many as 150 tramps per year were given shelter at the house during that era. Later still, the structure was used as a "pest house" to care for victims of typhoid fever. Finally, the residence was rented to individuals before being torn down in 1939. At the rear of this house were buried 30 or so of its one-time residents, including Elias Hutchins, a veteran of the War of 1812. The cemetery remains unmarked and all but forgotten. (Private Collection.)

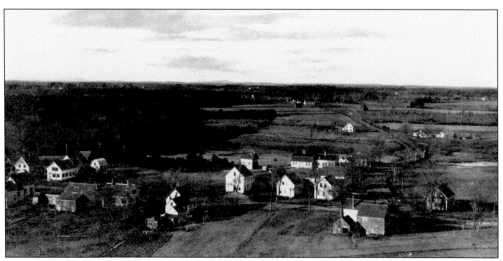

AERIAL VIEW. Seen in this photograph are High Street (running across the foreground) and Cat Mousam Road (extending off into the distance). The Poor Farm can be seen just off Cat Mousam Road behind the High Street homes. (It is the only building with a gambrel roof.) (84.L.122.2.)

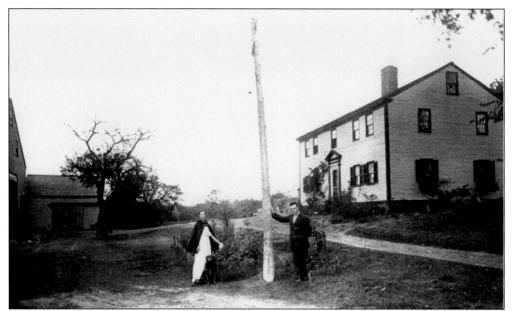

MOSES LITTLEFIELD HOMESTEAD. The home of Moses Littlefield, a Revolutionary War soldier, was built in 1758. When Moses passed away, he was interred on a hill adjacent to the house. Over a century later, in 1947, the property was purchased to make way for the Maine Turnpike, and at that time Littlefield's grave was inadvertently destroyed. The hand-carved headstone of Moses Littlefield was found in 2004, when the turnpike was widened. The tombstone, which is now at the Brick Store Museum, reads, "In Memory of Capt. M. Littlefield who died May 12th 1828 A75."

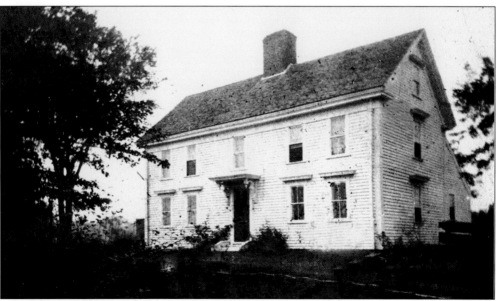

THE JOHN GILPATRIC HOMESTEAD. This home was built for Gilpatric in 1752, and it remained in the same family for over 100 years. The property eventually was sold to Emerson Littlefield, then to the Ryder family, and finally became the home of Ralph and Eldora Boston. The house was destroyed by fire on October 13, 1912. Lt. John Gilpatric, who served in the Revolutionary War, is buried in the cemetery located behind the former site of the house. (64.5.426.)

ACKNOWLEDGMENTS

Special thanks to the Brick Store Museum for the use of their images and collections—without them this book would not have been possible. Additional thanks to the staff of the Brick Store Museum, and to my coworkers, Roz Magnuson and Kathryn Hussey.

I would also like to thank Nelson Wentworth for loaning me photographs and books about his great-uncle John Coombs, but most importantly for his time and friendship.

To those folks of Alewive who eagerly shared their images and stories, many thanks. From them I realize that generosity and kindness are alive and well in Maine!

Additionally, this book would not have been possible without the following sources:
Kennebunk History, by George A. Gilpatric, 1939.
The Village of Kennebunk, by George A. Gilpatric, 1935.
History of Kennebunk, by Daniel Remich, 1911.
History of Wells and Kennebunk Maine, by E. E. Bourne, 1875.
An Architectural Walking Tour of the Kennebunks National Register Historic District, by Rosalind Magnuson, 1993.
Kennebunk Main Street, by Steven Burr, 1995.
The Ken Joy Scrapbooks at the Brick Store Museum.
The microfilm of the *York County Coast Star*, available at the Kennebunk Free Library and at the Brick Store Museum.
The Andrew Walker Diaries, at the Kennebunk Free Library.